T0312015

Cambridge Elements ≡

Elements on Women in the History of Philosophy
edited by
Jacqueline Broad
Monash University

CATHARINE TROTTER COCKBURN

Ruth Boeker
University College Dublin

Shaftesbury Road, Cambridge CB2 8EA, United Kingdom

One Liberty Plaza, 20th Floor, New York, NY 10006, USA

477 Williamstown Road, Port Melbourne, VIC 3207, Australia

314–321, 3rd Floor, Plot 3, Splendor Forum, Jasola District Centre, New Delhi – 110025, India

103 Penang Road, #05–06/07, Visioncrest Commercial, Singapore 238467

Cambridge University Press is part of Cambridge University Press & Assessment, a department of the University of Cambridge.

We share the University's mission to contribute to society through the pursuit of education, learning and research at the highest international levels of excellence.

www.cambridge.org
Information on this title: www.cambridge.org/9781009048682

DOI: 10.1017/9781009049160

© Ruth Boeker 2023

This publication is in copyright. Subject to statutory exception and to the provisions of relevant collective licensing agreements, no reproduction of any part may take place without the written permission of Cambridge University Press & Assessment.

First published 2023

A catalogue record for this publication is available from the British Library.

ISBN 978-1-009-04868-2 Paperback
ISSN 2634-4645 (online)
ISSN 2634-4637 (print)

Cambridge University Press & Assessment has no responsibility for the persistence or accuracy of URLs for external or third-party internet websites referred to in this publication and does not guarantee that any content on such websites is, or will remain, accurate or appropriate.

Catharine Trotter Cockburn

Elements on Women in the History of Philosophy

DOI: 10.1017/9781009049160
First published online: June 2023

Ruth Boeker
University College Dublin
Author for correspondence: Ruth Boeker, ruth.boeker@ucd.ie

Abstract: This Element offers the first detailed study of Catharine Trotter Cockburn's philosophy and covers her contributions to philosophical debates in epistemology, metaphysics, moral philosophy, and philosophy of religion. It examines not only Cockburn's view that sensation and reflection are the sources of knowledge, but also how she draws attention to the limitations of human understanding and how she approaches metaphysical debates through this lens. In the area of moral philosophy, this Element argues that it is helpful to take seriously Cockburn's distinction between questions concerning the metaphysical foundation of morality and questions concerning the practice of morality. Moreover, this Element examines Cockburn's religious views and considers her understanding of the relation between morality and religion and her religious views concerning the resurrection and the afterlife.

Keywords: Catharine Trotter Cockburn, early modern women philosophers, eighteenth-century British moral philosophy, human nature, metaphysics

© Ruth Boeker 2023

ISBNs: 9781009048682 (PB), 9781009049160 (OC)
ISSNs: 2634-4645 (online), 2634-4637 (print)

Contents

1 Catharine Trotter Cockburn's Life and Works

Catharine Trotter Cockburn was a remarkable playwright, writer, and philosopher. As a philosopher she contributed to a wide range of philosophical debates on issues in epistemology, metaphysics, moral philosophy, and religion.

1.1 Life and Career as Writer, Playwright, and Philosopher

Catharine Trotter (later Cockburn) was born in London in the 1670s, probably on 16 August 1679, as the second daughter of her parents David Trotter and Sarah Trotter (neé Ballenden).[1] Her parents were both Scottish. Her father David Trotter was a sea captain, working as commander for the Royal Navy, but unfortunately died in 1684. His death left the family in difficult financial circumstances. Sarah Trotter received a widow's pension from Charles II, but following the king's death in 1685, the family had to rely on the support of family and friends and her pension was not renewed until 1702 when Queen Anne acceded to the throne.[2] Catharine grew up under these financially challenging circumstances and is said to have largely educated herself. For instance, she taught herself how to write and to speak French 'without any instructor' (Birch 1751: 1:iv), but, as her biographer Thomas Birch notes, 'she had some assistance in the study of the *Latin* grammar and *Logic*' (Birch 1751: 1:iv–v).

She started writing at a young age and her literary writings include poetry, a novella, and five plays, which were all performed in London. Her first published work is an epistolary novella, *The Adventures of a Young Lady*, which she published anonymously in 1693 in *Letters of Love and Gallantry and Several Other Subjects, All Written by Ladies* (Briscoe 1693).[3] In 1695 her first play, *Agnes de Castro*, was performed and published in 1696. This was followed by *Fatal Friendship* (1698), *Love at a Loss* (1701), *The Unhappy Penitent* (1701), and *The Revolution of Sweden* (1706).[4] As Kelley (2004) notes, '[h]er drama is notable in this period for its unusually rational and politically aware female characters'. During these years Trotter also started to engage with

---

[1] According to her biographer, Thomas Birch (1751: 1:iv), she was born on 16 August 1679, but Kelley (2002: 1 n. 1) has found a church record that suggests that she was born five years earlier and baptized on 29 August 1674. However, there is also other evidence that points to a more likely birthdate in 1679. For instance, her gravestone states that she died 'in the 70 year of her age' (Kelley 2002: 1 n. 1). Moreover, Cockburn mentions in a letter to Pope from 1738 that she will soon turn 60 (British Library, Add. MS 4265, fol. 31, Broad (2021: 124 n. 7)). See also Kelley (2004, 2006b: vii).

[2] See Birch (1751: 1:iii–iv), Kelley (2004).

[3] This work was retitled *Olinda's Adventures, or, the Armours of a Young Lady* and reprinted by Briscoe under her name in 1718; it is also reprinted in Kelley (2006a).

[4] *Fatal Friendship* is the only play that was reprinted in her *Works*. See Kelley (2002) for further discussion. See also Bigold (2013: chs. 3 and 4).

the philosophical debates of her day and published her first philosophical work, *A Defence of Mr. Locke's Essay of Human Understanding*, in 1702, which I will discuss in Section 1.2.1.

Catharine Trotter was born into an Anglican family but converted to Catholicism at a young age. However, as she devoted more time to philosophical and religious studies and writing and as she also spent more time in philosophical and religious circles in London and Salisbury, she started to question her Catholic faith.[5] After thorough examination of both faiths, she converted back to Anglicanism in 1707 and published *A Discourse Concerning a Guide in Controversies* (*Works* 1:2–42) with a preface by Gilbert Burnet in the same year. This work outlines her criticism of the Roman Catholic Church. Gilbert Burnet, who was Bishop of Salisbury, his third wife, Elizabeth Berkeley Burnet, and Gilbert Burnet's cousin, Thomas Burnet of Kemnay,[6] played an important role in Cockburn's conversion back to the Church of England. Indeed, Elizabeth Berkeley Burnet went so far as to write to John Locke in June 1702 and to ask for his assistance to free her from 'a religion that puts such schacles on the exercise of thought and reason' (Locke 1976–89: letter 3153, 7:638).[7]

In 1708 Catharine married the clergyman Patrick Cockburn (1678–1749), and they moved from London to Nayland, Suffolk, the same year, but returned to London in 1713. Patrick Cockburn lost his appointment as curate when George I became king and Patrick refused to take the oath of abjuration. The subsequent years were financially challenging for the Cockburn family. After further consultation, Patrick Cockburn eventually agreed to take the oath in 1726 and was appointed as minister of the Episcopal Church in Aberdeen. They lived in Aberdeen for over a decade until Patrick was required to take up residence in Longhorsley in Northumberland in 1737. Catharine joined him there sometime between late 1738 and 1740.[8] Catharine and Patrick had four children: Sarah, Catharine, John, and Grissel.[9]

It is often thought that Cockburn's family duties left her little time for writing and that this explains why she did not publish any works between 1708 and 1726.[10] However, as Melanie Bigold (2013) notes, 'presenting Cockburn's writing from this print-oriented perspective is unfaithful to her lifelong

---

[5] For further details concerning these intellectual circles, see Bigold (2013: ch. 3) and Broad (2002: ch 6).

[6] Selections of Cockburn's correspondence with Thomas Burnet are included in her *Works*.

[7] Elizabeth Berkeley Burnet started corresponding with Locke in the 1690s. For further details, see Broad (2019: ch. 4).

[8] See Broad (2020: 189 n. 296).

[9] Her correspondence with Arbuthnot provides further insight into her family life (see Correspondence 125–253).

[10] For instance, see Birch (1751), Broad (2002: 156), Myers (1990: 164).

programme of reading and writing on literary, religious, and philosophical issues' (97). Bigold argues that it is important to consider Cockburn's unpublished manuscripts, in addition to her published works, to gain a fuller appreciation of her writings.[11] Bigold notes further that manuscript circulation was common in social and intellectual circles in eighteenth-century Britain and that not all manuscripts were intended for print publication. Moreover, Cockburn lacked the financial means to pay for publication costs herself and depended on patronage. Manuscript circulation helped her not only to share ideas, but also to find patrons to sponsor print publications (Bigold 2013: ch. 3).

Since I will comment further on her major published philosophical and religious works in the next section, I want to highlight here some of her other writings and correspondence that shed light on her philosophical thinking. Between 1731 and 1748 she was engaged in correspondence with her niece Ann Hepburn Arbuthnot. Cockburn takes on the role of mentor and encourages Arbuthnot's independent intellectual development and critical thinking.[12] Cockburn and Arbuthnot regularly exchange and discuss moral and religious books as well as novels and other literature. In their letters they discuss the moral philosophy of the Third Earl of Shaftesbury, Samuel Clarke, Joseph Butler, and various other philosophers. Additionally, Cockburn's correspondence with Thomas Sharp (*Works* 2:353–460)[13] and Edmund Law (Correspondence 254–65) sheds helpful light on her moral philosophy.

Although Cockburn rarely discusses the role of women in her published philosophical works, she was well aware of the challenges that women of her day faced, as her correspondence documents.[14] Moreover, in her 'Letter of Advice to Her Son' (*Works* 2:111–21), she argues for the equality of men and women and criticizes the unjust ways in which many men treat women:

> But do not imagine, that women are to be considered only as objects of your pleasure, as the fine gentlemen of the world seem, by their conduct, to do. There is nothing more unjust, more base, and barbarous, than is often practised towards them, under the specious names of love and gallantry; as if they had not an equal right, with those of the other sex, to be treated with justice and honour. (*Works* 2:119)

Cockburn continued her intellectual activities until the end of her life. She was well read in the philosophical and religious debates that took place in Britain during her day and engaged with them with wit and intellectual

---

[11] Cockburn's extant manuscripts can be found in the British Library, Add. MS 4264–7.

[12] See Cockburn, Correspondence 146, 149.

[13] For letters not included in her *Works*, see British Library, Add. MS 4264 and 4266.

[14] See also Broad (2014) and Hutton (2017) for further discussion of the challenges that women philosophers of the early modern period encountered.

sharpness, as her two major works in moral philosophy, *Remarks upon Some Writers* (1743) and *Remarks upon the Principles and Reasonings of Dr. Rutherforth's Essay* (1747), make evident. She died in Longhorsley on 11 May 1749 and is buried next to her husband Patrick, who died a few months earlier, and their youngest daughter Grissel, who died in 1742.

Unfortunately, Cockburn did not live long enough to see the publication of *The Works of Mrs. Catharine Cockburn*, edited by Thomas Birch, in 1751.[15] Cockburn played an active role in helping with the preparation of her *Works* when the project was started with the help and advice of her male mentors in the 1740s. This collection contains not only many of her previously published works, but also many of her works and writings that remained unpublished to that day.

1.2 Philosophical Works

1.2.1 A Defence of Mr. Locke's Essay of Human Understanding

Cockburn's first philosophical work was *A Defence of Mr. Locke's Essay of Human Understanding*, originally published anonymously in 1702. In this work Cockburn (then Trotter) takes on the charge of defending Locke against objections made in three anonymously published pamphlets, *Remarks upon an Essay Concerning Humane Understanding* (Anon. 1697a), *Second Remarks* (Anon. 1697b), and *Third Remarks* (Anon. 1699). Although it has been widely assumed that Thomas Burnet of Charterhouse was the author of these pamphlets,[16] Walmsley, Craig, and Burrows (2016) have offered convincing evidence that it is more likely that Richard Willis, successively bishop of Gloucester, Salisbury, and Winchester, was the author. Locke took note of the three pamphlets and made marginal notes in his copies of *Remarks* and *Third Remarks*.[17] However, he was not interested in responding publicly to them. Locke added 'An Answer to Remarks upon the Essay Concerning Human Understanding, &c.' (Locke 1823: 4:185–9) as a postscript to the publication of his reply to Edward Stillingfleet's letter.[18] Besides Locke's short dismissive remarks in this postscript, he did not engage again in print with *Remarks*, *Second Remarks*, or *Third Remarks*. In Cockburn's view the Remarker misunderstands and unfairly attacks Locke's *Essay*. Her *Defence* is not merely a 'defence' of Locke, but she

---

[15] Initially, William Warburton was meant to be the editor, but the project was handed over to Birch after Cockburn's death in 1749. See Bigold (2013: 94–5) for further details.

[16] This attribution has first been made by Birch (1751: xv).

[17] Locke's personal copies of these pamphlets with his marginalia can be found in the Beinecke Library, Yale University.

[18] Locke's public correspondence with Stillingfleet focuses on various metaphysical, epistemological, and religious issues (Locke 1823: vol. 4).

also builds on Lockean principles to develop clever arguments of her own that advance the philosophical debates of her day. As she puts it in one passage of her *Defence*, the question for her 'is not what Mr. *Locke* thinks, but what may be proved from his principles' (*Defence* 46). This intimates that she sees herself as a philosophical interlocutor among her philosophical contemporaries.

Cockburn's *Defence* covers a broad range of philosophical topics. She discusses epistemological questions concerning the origin of ideas. Like Locke, she rejects innate ideas and regards sensation and reflection as the sources of our ideas and the basis of moral and religious knowledge. She also engages with various other topics in moral philosophy such as the role of reward and punishment and the role of conscience. In other parts of *Defence* she turns to topics in metaphysics and religion such as questions concerning the immortality and immateriality of the soul, persons and personal identity, and the question whether thinking substances can be material.

Locke thought very favourably of *Defence* and was eager to identify the author of this anonymously published work (Locke 1976–89: letter 3234, 7:730–1). Eventually he learned that Cockburn was the author from their mutual friend Elizabeth Berkeley Burnet (Locke 1976–1989: letters 3153 and 3164, 7:638, 650–1). Locke expressed his gratitude in a letter of thanks to Cockburn (Locke 1976–1989: 7:730–1) and also sent her books and money in appreciation.

1.2.2 A Letter to Dr. Holdsworth

Cockburn's next major philosophical work was *A Letter to Dr. Holdsworth*, which she completed in 1724, but which was not published until January 1727. This work is a critical response to Winch Holdsworth's *A Sermon Preached before the University of Oxford on Easter Monday, 1719* (Holdsworth 1720). Cockburn believes that Holdsworth unfairly accused Locke of being a Socinian and of denying the resurrection of the same body.[19] In her *Letter to Holdsworth*, Cockburn aims to defend Locke against both of these charges. Socinians question the Trinity, because they believe that there is no scriptural basis for it, and they regard the doctrine as illogical. Holdsworth assumes that Locke denies the Trinity and thus regards him as a Socinian. Against Holdsworth's charge, Cockburn points out that Locke 'had not in his *Essay*, or any where else, written one word directly or indirectly concerning the Trinity' (*Letter to Holdsworth* 120). Cockburn's main focus in her *Letter to Holdsworth*, however,

---

[19] Socinianism is named after the sixteenth-century Italian theologian Faustus Socinus and refers to a theological movement that opposes the Trinity and Calvinist views. See Lucci (2021: ch. 2) for further discussion of Socinianism in the context of Locke's religious writings.

is to show that Locke, who was a careful reader of Scripture, argued for the resurrection of the dead, but not for the resurrection of the same body, because Scripture never mentions the resurrection of the same body. According to Cockburn, Locke's account of personal identity offers further support for his views concerning the resurrection, but she believes that Holdsworth has misunderstood Locke's thinking about identity and personal identity.

1.2.3 A Vindication of Mr. Locke's Christian Principles

Soon after the publication of Cockburn's *Letter to Holdsworth*, Holdsworth published *A Defence of the Resurrection of the Same Body* (1727) in response. This work has two parts. In Part I Holdsworth offers further 'proofs' that Locke was a Socinian, and Part II further explains Holdsworth's views concerning the resurrection of the same body. Cockburn was not satisfied with his response and wrote *A Vindication of Mr. Locke's Christian Principles* to further clarify Locke's and her view and to counter Holdsworth's position. Cockburn was not able to find a publisher for this work, and it was first published as part of her *Works* in 1751.

1.2.4 Remarks upon Some Writers

Cockburn completed another philosophical work, *Remarks upon Some Writers*, in 1740, but initially struggled to find a publisher willing to print her manuscript. This work was eventually published in August 1743 as part of *The History of the Works of the Learned* without her name on the title page. *Remarks upon Some Writers* begins with some 'Cursory Thoughts' (RSW 91–105) on metaphysical questions such as necessary existence, whether space is real and infinite, whether minds are extended and have a place in space. 'Cursory Thoughts' also contains a critical discussion of Isaac Watt's account of substance. The remaining parts of *Remarks upon Some Writers* focus on debates in British moral philosophy concerning the foundation of moral virtue and obligation. Cockburn critically engages with several authors who had criticized Samuel Clarke's moral philosophy. In particular, she challenges Edmund Law's Notes, which he added to his translation into English and edition of William King's *An Essay on the Origin of Evil* (Law 1732 [1731]),[20] John Gay's 'Preliminary Dissertation' (1732 [1731]), which was prefixed to Law's edition of King's *Essay on the Origin of Evil*, Thomas Johnson's *An Essay on Moral Obligation* (1731), George Johnston's *The Eternal Obligation of Natural Religion* (1732), and William Warburton's *Divine Legation of Moses* (1738).

---

[20] Here and in the following I cite from the second edition, because Cockburn used this edition.

Cockburn's *Remarks upon Some Writers* provides good insight into her own moral theory, which is based on human nature and moral fitnesses, and how she uses this theory not only to argue against theological voluntarism and self-interested moral views, but also to show that atheists can be virtuous.

1.2.5 Remarks upon the Principles and Reasonings of Dr. Rutherforth's Essay

After Thomas Rutherforth's publication of *An Essay on the Nature and Obligations of Virtue* (1744), Cockburn penned another work in response, which was published as *Remarks upon the Principles and Reasonings of Dr. Rutherforth's Essay* in 1747 with a preface by William Warburton. Cockburn rejects Rutherforth's self-interested moral view and argues instead that self-love should be distinguished from selfishness and that self-love and benevolence do not exclude each other (RR 158–9). In her view, there are plenty of instances of disinterested benevolence. She also presents several counter-examples to Rutherforth's view that virtue can be understood in terms of doing good to others (RR 151–5). For instance, she gives the example of a rich miser (RR 155) who saves up all his money to build a hospital after his death. Here we have an example of an action that does good to others, but in Cockburn's view it is not a virtuous action. Hence, the example is meant to show that some actions can do good to others without being virtuous. Contrary to Rutherforth, she argues that it is more plausible that 'virtue consists in acting suitably to the nature and relations of things' (RR 152). Furthermore, Cockburn examines the causes of moral obligation, free agency, and the role of the will of God. She also reflects on various other moral questions such as the relation between humans and non-human animals (RR 183–9, 212–3) and offers teleological consider-ations concerning the purpose of God's creatures.

1.3 Summary

In the following sections we will take a closer look at Cockburn's philosophy. Section 2 focuses on her epistemology and metaphysics and shows that she regards sensation and reflection as the sources of our ideas and knowledge. The section further highlights how Cockburn draws attention to the limitations of human understanding and how she approaches metaphysical debates – such as debates concerning persons and personal identity, the materiality or immateri-ality of the mind, God's necessary existence, or the metaphysical constitution of space – through this lens. Section 3 examines her moral philosophy and pays special attention to her metaphysics of morality and her views concerning the practice of morality, as well as her arguments against theological voluntarism, and her contribution to debates concerning self-interest and benevolence in British moral philosophy. Section 4 turns to her religious views and considers Cockburn's understanding of the relation between morality and religion, and her views concerning the resurrection and the afterlife. Section 5 highlights Cockburn's significant contributions to the philosophical debates of the early modern period and examines how her writings were received during the eighteenth century.

2 Epistemology and Metaphysics

Cockburn actively engaged with the epistemological and metaphysical debates of her day. Her epistemological views about the scope and the limitations of knowledge shape her metaphysical thinking. She engages with a range of debates in metaphysics, but her approach to all these debates is shaped by her awareness that human understanding is limited and that we are ignorant of many metaphysical facts. Section 2.1 introduces Cockburn's account of the sources, scope, and limitations of knowledge. Section 2.2 examines her contributions to philosophical debates about persons and personal identity, to the question whether minds must always be thinking, and to debates about whether minds or thinking substances are material or immaterial. Section 2.3 turns to Cockburn's contribution to metaphysical debates about God and the question whether he exists necessarily as well as to the question whether space exists and, if so, what kind of being it could be.

2.1 Knowledge and Its Limitations

2.1.1 Sources of Knowledge

Cockburn, like Locke, rejects innate ideas and principles (*Defence* 51–2, 59–60, 72–5, 79).[21] This means that she believes that initially there is no content in the mind and that the mind acquires content or ideas by means of sensation and reflection (*Defence* 40–1, 50–2, 59–60, 81). It is worth noting that neither Locke nor Cockburn deny that humans are born with mental capacities such as the capacity to have sensations, to reflect, or to reason. We can regard these mental capacities as dispositions that need to be developed and improved over time. Before we take a closer look at what role sensation and reflection play in Cockburn's epistemology, let us consider one of her arguments against innate ideas.

Cockburn believes that Locke's arguments sufficiently establish that there are no innate ideas and principles (*Defence* 51–2). Nevertheless, she offers further

---

[21] See Locke, *Essay* I. Principles for Locke and Cockburn have the form of a proposition and are composed of several ideas.

considerations of her own in response to objections that the Remarker raises against Locke's view. The Remarker proposes that infants may have innate ideas and these ideas can be excited as soon as a suitable occasion arises (*Second Remarks* 17). In response, Cockburn draws attention to the difference between ideas that are newly excited in the mind and ideas that have been retained in the mind and are revived at a later time (*Defence* 59–60). She challenges the Remarker's assumption that innate ideas are excited in the minds of children when a suitable occasion arises by asking what explains that children 'do not perceive, that they were in their minds before; but consider them as things new, and till then absolutely unknown to them' (*Defence* 59). By contrast, when ideas that a human being has formerly perceived are revived again at a later time, 'he considers them as things he is acquainted with, and clearly perceives they have been in his mind before' (*Defence* 59). Cockburn questions that there are innate ideas in the minds of infants, because she finds it implausible that one has no recollection that they have been in the mind before when one is conscious of them for the first time, and she regards this as 'one of the greatest arguments against *innate ideas*' (*Defence* 59). Furthermore, she finds it hard to conceive 'that innate ideas should need any objects to excite them; and that the mind should never excite any of them in itself without those objects; as it often does excite in itself the ideas it received by sensation, or reflection, without the presence of those objects, by which it first received them' (*Defence* 60). In Cockburn's view, these considerable differences between the supposed revival of innate ideas and the revival of ideas that have been previously acquired by sensation and reflection undermine the case for innate ideas and put the burden of proof on the Remarker or other defenders of innate ideas to offer a more plausible explanation.

Instead of relying on innate ideas, Cockburn claims that our ideas arise from sensation and reflection (*Defence* 40–1, 50, 52). So far her position appears Lockean,[22] and this is also how she presents it: 'it being clear to me, that whatever we can know at all, must be discoverable by Mr. *Locke*'s principles; for I cannot find any other way to knowledge, or that we have any one idea not derived from sensation and reflection' (*Defence* 40).

Despite the initial similarities, closer inspection brings to light that reflection plays a much broader role in her moral and religious epistemology than in Locke's philosophy.[23] For Locke, sensation and reflection are the two sources of ideas. He explains that sensation enables us to acquire ideas about external sensible objects such as the ideas of red, white, cold, warm, soft, hard, sweet,

---

[22] Locke argues in *Essay* II.i.3–4 that sensation and reflection are the only sources of simple ideas.
[23] This is noted in Sheridan (2006: 23). See also Sheridan (2007, 2022).

bitter, and other ideas of sensible qualities (*Essay* II.i.3). In Locke's view our mind is furnished with ideas not only by observing external objects; we can also turn inwards and observe our own mental operations by means of reflection. He introduces reflection as 'the *Perception of the Operations of our own Minds within us*' (*Essay* II.i.4). By means of reflection, he argues, we acquire ideas such as the ideas of perceiving, remembering, imagining, believing, hoping, desiring, and so on. By contrast, for Cockburn reflection is not restricted to observing mental operations within our own mind, and she extends the scope of reflection to include, for instance, reflection on human nature. In her philosophy, reflection on human nature plays a particularly important epistemological role and enables us to acquire moral knowledge and knowledge of God's attributes.[24] Since I will examine in Section 3, at greater length, how Cockburn's moral philosophy is grounded in her account of human nature, let me now turn to her discussion of our knowledge of God's attributes.

2.1.2 Knowledge of God's Attributes

As I will explain in Section 2.3.1, Cockburn believes that a first cause of all other beings necessarily exists (*Defence* 49–50, RSW 91–5). For the time being, let us take God's existence for granted and focus on the epistemological question, namely whether it is possible to acquire knowledge of God's attributes, if sensation and reflection are the only sources of ideas. This is a worry that the Remarker presents for Locke's philosophy:

> 'Tis not enough (as I judge) for our satisfaction, and to establish the certainty of Reveal'd Religion, that we know the Physical or Metaphysical Attributes of the Divine Nature: we must also know its Moral Attributes, as I may so call them; such as Goodness, Justice, Holiness, and particularly Veracity. Now, these I am not able to deduce or make out from your Principles. You have prov'd very well an Eternal, All-powerful, and All-knowing-Being: but how this supreme Being will treat us, we cannot be assur'd from these Attributes. (*Remarks* 7)

The Remarker is particularly concerned how Locke is able to establish God's veracity without appeal to innate ideas. Before I take a closer look at Cockburn's response to the Remarker's worry concerning veracity, let us consider how, according to Cockburn, we acquire knowledge of God's other moral attributes

---

[24] For further discussion of Cockburn's moral and religious epistemology, see Sheridan (2007, 2022), Waithe (1987–95: 3:107–17). It may be worth mentioning another difference with Locke's epistemology. According to Locke, sensation and reflection are the two sources of simple ideas, but sensation or reflection do not directly result in knowledge. Locke understands knowledge as the perception of the agreement or disagreement of ideas (*Essay* IV.i.2), and this involves the comparison of two or more ideas.

such as his goodness or justice. In her view, God's moral attributes have to be considered in relation to '*the natural good or evil of his creatures*' (*Defence* 44). She assumes that the nature of God's creatures resembles his nature, because God 'cannot will any thing contrary to his nature' (*Defence* 43). This leads her to argue that in order to acquire knowledge of God's moral attributes we have to reflect upon our own nature:

> for whatever is the original standard of good and evil, it is plain, we have no notion of them but by their conformity, or repugnancy to our reason, and with relation to our nature; and that what according to it we perceive to be good, we ascribe to the Supreme Being; for we cannot know, that the nature of God is good, before we have a notion of good. It must be then by reflecting upon our own nature, and the operations of our minds, that we come to know the nature of God. (*Defence* 44)

As this passage makes explicit, Cockburn believes that before we can have an idea of God's goodness, we must have an idea of good, which we acquire by reflecting on our own nature. Furthermore, it shows that reflection is a central epistemic principle in her philosophy and that reflection on human nature, in particular, equips us with important ideas.

On this basis, let us turn to the question of whether and how it is possible to acquire knowledge of God's veracity without appeal to innate ideas. This question is particularly pressing since it is not obvious whether we can acquire the idea of veracity as well as the related idea of perfection by means of sensation and reflection.[25] According to Locke's critics, it is more plausible to consider these ideas as innate, but Cockburn rejects this and offers an alternative explanation.

Cockburn agrees with the Remarker's view that veracity is ascribed to God, because it is a perfection (*Defence* 49). Yet she raises a further question, namely on what grounds is one justified in concluding 'that whatever is a perfection must be in God' (*Defence* 49)? Cockburn accepts neither the possible response that it is an innate principle nor the possible reponse that God's perfection is a brute fact. Instead she argues that anyone who attentively reflects on how the mind acquires knowledge of God will realize that perfection is not part of our initial idea of God. Rather, once we have 'discovered a first being, the source of all others, and what attributes we must necessarily ascribe to him, as such, we perceive, that to admit any imperfection in him would be a contradiction to our first necessary conceptions of him' (*Defence* 49).[26] Otherwise, if the first being was imperfect, then there could 'be a more perfect being, than the eternal source of all Being' (*Defence* 50). In her view such a supposition is absurd and, thus, it

---

[25] For further discussion, see Sund (2013: 46–50).   [26] See also Cockburn, *Defence* 45.

cannot be doubted 'that the eternal source of all being must exist in the most perfect manner possible' (*Defence* 50).

She acknowledges that this response may not satisfy the Remarker, since the Remarker expects Locke to tell us what he means by perfection and 'how it is deriv'd from the Senses, and how it includes Veracity' (*Remarks* 8).[27] However, as Cockburn quickly notes, the problem with this statement is that the Remarker neglects 'that Mr. *Locke* has another principle of knowledge, which he calls *reflection*' (*Defence* 50).

In Cockburn's view, it is possible to explain 'how the idea of perfection ... may be derived from *sensation* and *reflection*' (*Defence* 50). First of all, we have to perceive 'in ourselves some *powers and faculties*, as of *knowing, willing, moving*, &c and of particular actions, and general abstract ideas' (*Defence* 50). Once we have a pool of these various ideas in our minds we can compare them with each other and start to realize that some of them 'are congruous, and others repugnant to each other, and to our reason' (*Defence* 50). Furthermore, she argues that 'we know, that some things are better than others' (*Defence* 50) and that we may only be able to grasp fractions of power, knowledge, and goodness, since we are finite beings with limited mental capacities. This leads her to conclude that: 'these things may be far more extensive, even to all that can exist. And the highest possible degree of these, which we find it better to have, than to be without, that we call perfection; which to have an adequate idea of, we must comprehend the existence of an infinite spirit' (*Defence* 50).

Cockburn's explanation rests on two assumptions: first, that we can grasp what is good and evil and, second, that we compare ideas or things and regard some as better than others. If we take any thing that we regard as good, we can imagine another thing that is even better. If we repeat this process, Cockburn believes, we will eventually acquire the idea of perfection.

Having explained how we can acquire the idea of perfection by means of sensation and reflection, Cockburn turns to the other part of the Remarker's question, namely how perfection includes veracity (*Defence* 50–1).[28] She challenges the Remarker to explain 'upon what grounds veracity is to him a perfection' (*Defence* 51). To argue that veracity is a perfection because God is veracious, would be to argue in a circle (*Defence* 51). Thus, Cockburn maintains, the Remarker 'must then know, that veracity is a perfection from some other rule; and here I am afraid he will be involved in great difficulty; *for the truth of our faculties*, he says, *depends on the veracity of their author*' (*Defence* 51). In these passages Cockburn draws attention to a sceptical challenge, namely that in order to establish that God is veracious, we need to rely on our cognitive capacities. However, to know that our

---

[27] Quoted in Cockburn, *Defence* 50.   [28] See also Anon., *Remarks* 8.

cognitive capacities are veridical, we have to presuppose God's veracity.[29] In her view, there is no easy way out for the Remarker who may quickly be trapped in 'an incurable scepticism' (*Defence* 51).

Nevertheless, Cockburn believes that there is a way out, and she acknowledges 'two ways of knowing that veracity is a perfection' (*Defence* 51). One option is that 'it is an innate principle, originally imprinted on the mind' (*Defence* 51). She does not elaborate on this possibility, because she believes that Locke has convincingly shown that there are no innate ideas and principles. The other option is that we discover that veracity is a perfection by means of sensation and reflection (*Defence* 52). This is the option Cockburn favours. To convince her opponent, she offers several examples that appear intuitively certain such as that truth differs from falsehood, 'that doing a thing differs from not doing it; that an apple . . . is not a horse; that pain is not pleasure; and that performing a promise is not breaking it' (*Defence* 52).[30] According to Cockburn, we are able to recognize not only that things are different but also that some things are better than others. For instance, 'performing our promise, *i.e.* veracity, is more agreeable to our nature, and beneficial to mankind, than the contrary' (*Defence* 52). On this basis, she believes that it is possible to use Lockean principles to establish that veracity is a perfection:

> if in Mr. *Locke*'s way we can know, that what is beneficial to mankind, is better than what is destructive to it; that happiness is better than misery, that power and knowledge is better than impotence and ignorance; if we may trust our faculties in discerning truths, as sensible to us as our own existence; it cannot be doubted, that in his way we can be assured, that veracity is a perfection, till some other reason of falsehood can be imagined, than ignorance, impotence, or willing evil for its own sake, which cannot be conceived possible. (*Defence* 52)

The above considerations not only show how Cockburn establishes that we can acquire knowledge of God's moral attributes on the basis of sensation and reflection but also shed light on her argumentative strategy: by identifying problems for the view of her opponent and by showing how her own view offers a better solution, she undermines the view of her opponent and puts the burden of proof on them to defend their views against the problems she raised.

2.1.3 Limitations of Knowledge

Cockburn is not sceptical about our ability to acquire knowledge. Indeed, she accepts that we can have moral knowledge and knowledge of the existence of

---

[29] The problem that Cockburn raises here is similar to the so-called Cartesian Circle that has been raised for Descartes's arguments in *Meditations* 3 and 4 (AT VII:34–62; CSM II:24–43).

[30] Locke would regard these as examples of intuitive knowledge. See Locke, *Essay* IV.ii.1.

God and his attributes. However, she is also attentive to the fact that human capacities are limited and that we are ignorant about many metaphysical facts.[31] In this vein, she writes that 'it has long been my opinion, that, from our ignorance of the nature of things, or of their manner of acting, how they cease to act, or how they resume their actions, no other reasonable conclusion can be drawn, but of the narrowness of our understandings' (RSW 101). Cockburn's view that the human understanding is very limited finds clear expression in her account of the human mind. For her a mind, or – as she also calls it – a soul, is a substance that thinks, but we are not in a position to know its exact metaphysical constitution and, in particular, we are not in a position to know whether minds are material or immaterial entities (*Defence* 60–1, 66, 69, 83–4, RSW 103). She accepts that we have access to mental operations and that 'we have no idea of the soul but by her operations' (*Defence* 60), but we lack access to metaphysical entities that underlie these mental operations. Moreover, she finds it 'very intelligible' that mind and body interact, 'yet how it is possible for thought to excite motion, and to be excited by it, is utterly inconceivable to us' (*Works* 2:134).

The important point for Cockburn is that our lack of such metaphysical knowledge does not undermine morality and religion. For instance, she argues that our ignorance of whether human minds are material or immaterial does not weaken religious beliefs in immortality (*Defence* 53–7, 60–9, 81, RSW 103).[32] In her view it is unproblematic that our metaphysical knowledge is limited; it reveals that God wisely created human faculties and proportioned them to our needs:

> Our wise Maker has proportioned our faculties only to our necessities, and has made his will known to us by a light of nature clear enough to render any one inexcusable, who does not follow it; tho' the full assurance of an eternal retribution is only given us by *Jesus Christ, who has brought life, and immortality, to light, through the Gospel*, which I have already shown, that Mr. *Locke*'s principles give us a sure foundation for, both of natural and revealed religion. (*Defence* 69)

Cockburn is not troubled by the limitations of our metaphysical knowledge, because this enables us to devote more time to morality and religion. Let us now see how her view that our metaphysical knowledge is limited shapes her approach to the study of the human mind and several other topics in metaphysics.

---

[31] See Cockburn, Correspondence 148, *Defence* 60, 62–3, 66, 69, 81, RSW 96–7, 99–102, 104–5.
[32] Locke makes a similar claim in *Essay* IV.iii.6.

2.2 Persons, Souls, Immortality, and Immateriality

2.2.1 Persons and Personal Identity

In 1694 Locke added a new chapter to the second edition of his *Essay* titled 'Of Identity and Diversity' (II.xxvii). In this chapter Locke develops a novel account of persons and personal identity and emphasizes the importance of distinguishing the idea of a person from the idea of a man or human being, as we may prefer to say today, and from the idea of a substance.[33] For Locke a person is 'a thinking intelligent Being, that has reason and reflection, and can consider itself as it self, the same thinking thing in different times and places' (*Essay* II.xxvii.9). He argues further that persons are moral agents, who will be held accountable for their actions (*Essay* II.xxvii.26), and believes that persons, rather than human beings or substances, will continue to exist in the afterlife. Locke claims repeatedly that personal identity over time consists in sameness of consciousness and personal identity does not have to coincide with the continued existence of a human being or the continued existence of a substance (*Essay* II.xxvii.9–26).

Locke's account of persons and personal identity was widely discussed soon after its publication. Several of Locke's early critics, including the anonymous author of *Remarks*, worry that his view undermines the immateriality and the immortality of the soul (*Remarks* 8–14, *Second Remarks* 9–10, 13–17, *Third Remarks* 16–25).[34] Often these accusations arise because Locke's critics fail to take seriously his distinctions between the ideas of person, man, and substance, and they simply assume that a person has to be an immaterial substance.[35] Locke resists such metaphysical assumptions, because he believes that our knowledge of the metaphysical constitution of things is extremely limited. For instance, he claims that we cannot know whether finite thinking substances are material or immaterial.[36] Moreover, for Locke it is irrelevant to show that persons are immaterial substances, because there can be personal identity, namely sameness of consciousness, without the continued existence of an immaterial substance.

Cockburn was a more careful reader of Locke than many of his early critics and notices that the Remarker fails to acknowledge the Lockean distinctions between the ideas of person, man, and soul or substance (*Defence* 55).[37] As

---

[33] For detailed discussions of Locke's account of persons and personal identity, see Boeker (2021a, 2021b), Thiel (2011).

[34] See also Boeker (2021b: ch. 10), Thiel (2011, 2012).

[35] Although the terms 'soul' and 'immaterial substance' are sometimes used interchangeably, Locke (and some of his contemporaries), use the term 'soul' to refer to a thinking substance, irrespective of whether it is material or immaterial. See Locke (1823: 4:33–7).

[36] See Locke, *Essay* II.xxiii.28–32, 37, IV.iii.6, Locke (1823: 4:33–7).

[37] For further discussion of Cockburn's contribution to philosophical debates on persons and personal identity, see Boeker (2021b: ch. 10), Broad (2002: 153–5), De Tommaso and Mocchi (2021), Gordon-Roth (2015a), Ready (2002), Thomas (2015), Waithe (1987–95: 3:117–21).

a result, the Remarker struggles to make sense of some of Locke's examples. For instance, the Remarker queries whether and how a person or soul can think apart from the man (*Second Remarks* 15). As Cockburn points out in response, the difficulty arises because the Remarker equates the terms 'soul', 'man', and 'person'. If all of these terms are used interchangeably, then it does not make sense to ask how a person or soul can think apart from the man, because then the question becomes 'whether the soul thinking apart, what the soul is not conscious of, be not a distinct soul from the soul' (*Defence* 55). Such a question is absurd to ask. Since Locke neither equates the idea of a person nor the idea of a soul with the idea of a man, it is meaningful to ask whether a person can continue to exist and think apart from a man. Thus, he does not have to worry about the problems that the Remarker raises.

It is worth taking a closer look at Cockburn's comments on the Lockean distinction between the ideas of a person and a man. She explains it as follows:

> But understanding by *person*, as he does, *self consciousness*, and by *man* the *soul and body united*, he may question, whether the *same soul*, the *same permanent substance*, thinking *apart from the body* in sound sleep, what the waking *man* is not conscious of, whether that *incommunicable consciousness* does not make the *soul*, and the *man* consisting of body and soul, two distinct persons; *personal identity*, according to him, consisting in the *same consciousness*, and not in the same *substance*: for whatever substance there is, without *consciousness* there is no *person*. *Consciousness* therefore, and not *substance*, making a *person*, the same consciousness must make the same person, whether in the same, or in different substances; and no farther than the same consciousness extends, can there be the same person: but wherever there are *two distinct incommunicable consciousnesses*, there are two distinct *persons*, though in the same substance. (*Defence* 55–6)

Although Cockburn and Locke are in agreement that it is important to distinguish the idea of a person from the idea of a man, it is worth noting that Cockburn's explanation of the meaning of 'person' and 'man' diverges from Locke's own understanding of these terms.[38] Cockburn interprets Locke as meaning 'by *person* ... *self consciousness*' (*Defence* 55). Her interpretation differs from the definition that Locke gives of a person in *Essay* II.xxvii.9, where he describes a person as 'a thinking intelligent Being, that has reason and reflection, and can consider it self as it self, the same thinking thing in different times and places'.

This has prompted Jessica Gordon-Roth (2015a) to propose that, for Cockburn, Lockean persons are modes, while it is questionable that Locke

---

[38] This point is noted in Gordon-Roth (2015a: 71). See Locke, *Essay* II.xxvii.9, 26, for his characterizations of the idea of a person, and *Essay* II.xxvii.6–8, 21, for his understanding of the idea of a man (or human being).

himself regards persons as modes.[39] Interpreters who ascribe a mode interpretation to Cockburn tend to assume that she adopts Locke's understanding of substances and modes. However, this is not straightforward. Locke's understanding of modes is peculiar and was not widely shared by his and Cockburn's contemporaries.[40] Rather than taking for granted that Cockburn shares Locke's ontological classifications, further investigation is needed into whether or not she adopts them. If she does not share Locke's view, it remains to consider whether her own view is similar to more traditional ontological classifications.

Locke argues that complex ideas can be divided into ideas of substances, ideas of modes, and ideas of relations (*Essay* II.xii.3), and he accepts that ideas of substances denote substances, ideas of modes denote modes, and – though this is controversial – ideas of relations denote relations.[41] While several other philosophers identify modes with properties, Lockean modes are not restricted to properties. Throughout the *Essay* Locke gives various examples of ideas of modes, which include the following: triangle; gratitude; murder; number; beauty; rainbow; modes of thinking such as sensation, remembrance, contemplation, attention, or dreaming; and various modes of action such as running or speaking.[42] For Locke, any complex idea that does not denote a substance or relation denotes a mode.

There is not sufficient textual evidence for assuming that Cockburn shares Locke's peculiar understanding of modes. An alternative possibility is that she adopts metaphysical categories that include essential properties or principal attributes in addition to modes and substances.[43] In support of this reading one can draw attention to the fact that she mentions at the beginning of her *Remarks upon Some Writers* that, according to Samuel Clarke, different natures 'are distinguished one from another by a diversity, not only of *modes*, but also of *essential attributes*' (RSW 91). Although we cannot be certain that she speaks

---

[39] De Tommaso (2017: 336) and De Tommaso and Mocchi (2021: 217) mention Gordon-Roth's mode interpretation. De Tommaso and Mocchi (2021: 217) argue that Cockburn accepts a non-substance view of persons. Locke interpreters have not settled whether persons are modes or substances. Law (1769) and LoLordo (2011, 2012) defend the view that Lockean persons are modes, but Gordon-Roth (2015b), Rickless (2015), and Winkler (1991) challenge it and argue instead that Lockean persons are substances. For an intermediate position, see Leisinger (2019). Another option, mentioned by Anstey (2013), Atherton (2013), and Boeker (2021b), is that Locke remains agnostic whether persons are modes or substances.

[40] For helpful discussion of Locke's account of modes, see LoLordo (2013; 2012: 74–82).

[41] Rickless (2017) argues that Locke is a realist about relations.

[42] See Locke, *Essay* II.xii.4–5, II.xvi, II.xviii.4, II.xix.1, II.xxii.10.

[43] In *Principles* I.53 Descartes (AT VIIIA:25; CSM I:210–11) claims that each substance has exactly one principal attribute. In the following, I do not assume that Cockburn shares this metaphysical commitment. Instead, other philosophers may argue that it is possible that a substance has more than one essential attribute. Indeed, Cockburn considers this possibility in *Defence* 60–1.

in her own voice, since the passage in question explains Clarke's view, the fact that she does not distance herself from his position intimates that she finds it plausible that substances have not only modes but also essential properties or attributes.[44]

If it is correct that Cockburn acknowledges essential properties or attributes as a metaphysical category in addition to modes and substances, then the question – discussed by interpreters of Cockburn – of whether she regards Lockean persons as modes or substances overlooks a further option, namely the possibility that for Cockburn Lockean persons are essential properties. This option has not been discussed so far, since interpreters have not yet taken seriously the possibility that Cockburn's metaphysics includes different ontological categories than Locke's. However, how likely is it actually that Cockburn would regard Lockean persons as essential properties rather than modes? She claims that Locke identifies a person with self-consciousness. Whether a person in this sense is a mode or an essential property depends on an ambiguity of the term 'self-consciousness'. If self-consciousness refers to individual self-conscious states, then it is more plausible to understand it as a mode, since individual self-conscious states change. Alternatively, if self-consciousness refers to the ability to be self-conscious, then the possibility that it is an essential property becomes a more viable option.

2.2.2 Souls, Thinking, and Immortality

Let us turn to the Remarker's worry that Locke's view undermines a proof of the immortality of the soul (*Remarks* 8) and analyse Cockburn's response. Although Locke believes that persons will continue to exist in the afterlife, this is a matter of faith for him rather than knowledge, and thus, as Cockburn rightly points out (*Defence* 54), he neither attempted nor intended to *prove* the immortality of a person or soul.[45] Nevertheless, the Remarker accuses Locke of making two assumptions, namely, first, the assumption that the soul does not always think and, second, the assumption that matter can think. According to the Remarker, both of these assumptions undermine the immortality of the soul (*Remarks* 8). Cockburn finds the Remarker's reasoning hard to follow. She notes that she does not see how the assumption that the soul does not always think is meant to be relevant 'at all to the proofs of the immortality of the soul' (*Defence* 53). She asks: 'Do they depend upon the contrary supposition, that the

---

[44] She also invokes essential properties in her discussion of the thinking matter hypothesis in *Defence* 61, which is the topic of Section 2.3. For further discussion of her defence of the thinking matter hypothesis, see Boeker (2021b: 222–4).

[45] See Locke, *Essay* IV.xviii.7.

soul *always thinks*?' (*Defence* 53). For Cockburn it is neither plausible to base proofs of immortality on the assumption that the soul always thinks nor on the contrary assumption that the soul does not always think, because none of them provides a solid foundation for immortality.

In the following I want to focus more closely on the question of whether there has to be a perpetually thinking soul, as the Remarker and several of Locke's early critics argue.[46] Their worry is the following: given Locke's view that personal identity consists in sameness of consciousness, a person's existence over time can have gaps. If a person stops thinking and ceases to be conscious, for instance during dreamless sleep, then it seems that the person ceases to exist when she stops thinking. Moreover, it is unclear how she can be recreated after a period without thoughts and instead it may be more likely that a *new* person comes into existence. This is not merely a concern during life on Earth but is also conceived to be a threat to the possibility of the afterlife.

The Remarker struggles to comprehend how there can be 'a *thoughtless, senseless, lifeless Soul*' (*Second Remarks* 16) and presses Locke to explain how a soul can start thinking again after a period without thoughts:

> However, you ought to tell us, how you bring the Soul out of this unintelligible State. What Cause can you assign able to produce the first Thought at the end of this Sleep and Silence, in a total Ecclipse and intermission of Thinking? Upon your Supposition, That all our Thoughts perish in sound Sleep, and all Cogitation is extinct, we seem to have a new Soul every Morning. (*Second Remarks* 16–17)

Here the Remarker draws attention to the absurd consequences of Locke's views and maintains that if thinking stops at night, then a new soul will have to come into existence. This argument is meant to offer indirect support for the view that the soul always thinks.

Cockburn does not find this objection convincing and counters it with a series of clever arguments of her own (*Defence* 53–60). First of all, she draws attention to the fact that we have very limited understanding of how our mental operations work. She writes:

> If that be a good argument, we must deny the most common and visible operations in nature. Do you understand *how* your soul thinks at all? *How* it passes from one thought to another? *How* it preserves its treasure of ideas, to produce them at pleasure on occasions? And recollects those it had not in a long time reflected on? *How* it moves your body, or is affected by it? These are operations, which I suppose you are not so sceptical as to doubt of; nor yet to pretend to understand how they are done. (*Defence* 57)

---

[46] For further discussion, see Boeker (2021b: 211–24), Gordon-Roth (2015a), Thomas (2015).

Second, she offers a *reductio* argument that is meant to show the strange consequences that follow if one accepts the Remarker's assumption that a new soul comes into existence each morning after unconscious sleep (*Defence* 58). As Cockburn points out, anyone who worries how the soul starts to think again after a night of sleep should likewise worry how the soul transitions from one thought to the next, because we lack insight not only into how we start thinking again after a night of sleep, but also about how one thought follows another. For instance, let us suppose that at one moment you are thinking about Cockburn's philosophy, and the next you consider what you would like to eat for dinner. What explains the transition from your thought about philosophy to your thought about dinner? Cockburn's point is that if one accepts the Remarker's assumption that a new soul comes into existence each morning after unconscious sleep, then by the same token one will also have to accept that a new soul comes into existence whenever there is a transition from one thought to another. Since this is an absurd consequence, she believes that the Remarker's assumption should be rejected. Cockburn's argument can be summarized and analysed as follows:

(1) Assume a new soul comes into existence each morning after unconscious sleep.

(2) If (1) is correct, then we will also have to accept that a new soul comes into existence each time the soul has a new thought.

(3) Hence, a new soul comes into existence each time the soul has a new thought.

(4) This is absurd. Consequently, (1) is problematic.

Cockburn further challenges an analogy that the Remarker draws between thinking and motion. This analogy is meant to provide further support for the Remarker's point that, upon Locke's view, a new soul comes into existence each morning after unconscious sleep. The Remarker presents the analogy as follows:

> If a Body cease to move, and come to perfect rest, the Motion it had cannot be restor'd, but a new Motion may be produc'd. If all Cogitation be extinct, all our Ideas are extinct, so far as they are Cogitations, and seated in the Soul: So we must have them new imprest; we are, as it were, new born, and begin the World again. (*Second Remarks*, 17)

Cockburn acknowledges that we can consider motion in bodies as analogous to thought or cogitation in the soul (*Defence* 58). However, she points out that the fact that a new thought has come into existence does not entail that a new soul has also come into existence. Likewise, it does not follow from the fact that there is a new motion that a new body has come into existence. Therefore she rejects the Remarker's unjustified metaphysical conclusion and argues for a more modest result instead: 'all I can infer from this parallel, is, that my thoughts today are not the same numerical thoughts I had yesterday; which, I believe, nobody supposes they are, though they did not suspect they had a *new soul* with every *new thought*' (*Defence* 58).

To sum up, we have seen that Cockburn offers several good arguments of her own that undermine the assumption that the soul must always think.

2.2.3 Materiality and Immateriality

To gain insight into Cockburn's thinking about the metaphysical constitution of finite substances such as minds and bodies, it is helpful to consider how she responds to another charge that the Remarker raised against Locke's philosophy. Locke's thinking matter hypothesis, namely the hypothesis that it is possible that material entities can think, sparked much controversy among his contemporaries.[47] The Remarker rejects it and insists that minds must be immaterial substances (*Remarks* 8, 13–14, *Third Remarks* 16–25). In the following I will provide further background to this dispute, take a closer look at the Remarker's objection, and then show how Cockburn responds with a clever dilemma that undermines immaterialist views of the mind.

As we have already seen in Section 2.1.3, Cockburn, like Locke, is cautious not to make claims about the metaphysical constitution of mind and body that exceed the boundaries of human understanding. Locke argues that we have access to our various experiences such as feeling hungry, feeling cold, believing that Paris is the capital of France, or remembering last week's dinner party. Moreover, he argues that experiences do not freely float around, but rather inhere in some underlying substance, but we are not in a position to know whether this underlying substance is material or immaterial (Locke 1823: 4:33–7). On this basis he argues for the hypothesis that it is possible that systems of matter have been given the power to think (*Essay* IV.iii.6).

Locke's thinking matter hypothesis troubles the Remarker for a number of reasons. For instance, the Remarker worries that Locke's view undermines proofs of the immortality of the soul (*Remarks* 9), that it threatens human agency and free will (*Third Remarks* 18–20), and that this 'would pervert all our rules in Moral Philosophy' (*Third Remarks* 20). Here I want to focus on a further metaphysical worry that the Remarker raises, namely the problem of how the soul or mind can be distinguished or individuated from material objects or nothingness if the soul or mind is material and does not always think. The Remarker presents this problem as follows:

---

[47] For further discussion, see Boeker (2021b: 224–43), Bolton (2016), Duncan (2022), Jolley (2015: ch. 5), Kim (2019: ch. 4), Yolton (1983).

> What is the Soul when she does not think? what Idea or Definition can you give of her in that State? she must be actually something if she exist. She must then have some Properties whereby she may be defin'd or describ'd; something whereby she is distinguish'd from Nothing, and from Matter. (*Remarks* 9)

It is important for the Remarker to distinguish souls from matter and nothingness. The Remarker believes that thinking is an essential property that souls have and that makes it possible to distinguish them from matter and nothingness. Taking into consideration the Remarker's view that the property of thinking is the feature that makes a soul a soul and distinguishes it from other types of entities offers further insight into why it is so important for the Remarker that the soul always thinks: if a soul stopped thinking, it would cease to be a soul. These considerations also shed light on why the Remarker is attracted to a dualist view, according to which minds and bodies are distinct types of substances.

On this basis, let us turn to Cockburn's response.[48] She is willing to assume the Remarker's view for the sake of argument and then constructs a dilemma for the Remarker and other philosophers attracted to immaterialist accounts of the mind. Her argument can be analysed as follows:

(1) Assume souls must always think, because thinking is an essential property that distinguishes souls from other material substances and from nothingness.

(2) There are two options: either souls have other essential properties in addition to thinking or they do not and thinking is the only essential property of souls.

(3) If souls do not have any other essential properties, then there is no reason why matter may not have the power to think.

(4) If souls have other essential properties, then these other properties distinguish souls from matter and nothingness, and it is unproblematic if souls do not always think.

(5) Hence, assumption (1) is mistaken.

Cockburn offers an indirect argument that is meant to show the falsity of the Remarker's assumption, stated in premise (1). Her argumentative strategy is clever: she considers two exclusive options and shows that each option undermines the Remarker's position. On the one hand, if it is the case that souls do not have any other essential properties besides thinking, then there is no reason why souls must be immaterial, because there is nothing that rules out the possibility

---

[48] See Cockburn, *Defence* 60–1.

that a soul could be a material thinking being. On the other hand, if souls have other essential properties in addition to thinking, then there is no need to postulate that souls must always think, because the other essential properties are sufficient to distinguish souls from matter and nothingness. Cockburn's argument brings to light that the Remarker's view rests on dogmatic assumptions. She shows that both the assumption that souls must be immaterial and the assumption that they must be always thinking lack support. Her argument also challenges the assumption that souls (and other substances) have only one essential property. Her willingness to question dogmatic metaphysical assumptions opens space for other metaphysical possibilities and teaches us to investigate all these options.

2.3 God, Substances, and Space

Cockburn begins her *Remarks upon Some Writers* (1743) with 'a few cursory thoughts' (RSW 89) on several metaphysical controversies among her contemporaries such as questions concerning necessary existence, the reality and infinity of space, the extension and location of souls or thinking substances, and Isaac Watt's peculiar account of substances[49] (RSW 91–105).[50] Although she regards these debates as 'abstruse controversies' (RSW 89), she nevertheless believes that it is worth examining them, since they are 'subjects of universal concernment' (RSW 90). In the following, we will take a closer look at her discussion of God's necessary existence (Section 2.3.1) and space (Section 2.3.2).

2.3.1 God and Necessary Existence

Cockburn accepts that God exists on the basis of a version of the cosmological argument for God's existence.[51] Although there are different versions of cosmological arguments, they commonly argue that there has to be a first cause of all other things that exist and regard this first cause as God. Since Cockburn describes God as 'a first being, the source of all others' (*Defence* 49), 'the first cause' (RSW 92, 93, 103), 'the cause of all other beings' (RSW 92), or as 'an intelligent first cause of all beings' (RR 168), we have evidence that she endorses a cosmological argument for God's existence. She seems to accept that all things that exist must have a cause, because something cannot come into existence from nothing. This leads her to infer that a first cause, namely God,

---

[49] See Watts (1733).

[50] These sections are often referred to as 'Cursory Thoughts', as Cockburn does in the full title and preface of RSW.

[51] For further discussion, see Lascano (2019).

must exist. Her inference to the conclusion that there is a first cause rests on the implicit premise that there cannot be an infinite series of causes and effects. Cockburn was probably aware of this, since a similar argument can be found in Edmund Law's Notes, which Cockburn studied in detail. Law regards the possibility that there is an infinite series of causes as 'absurd' (Law 1732 [1731]: Note 10, 46), and Cockburn does not argue for an alternative position. Thus, we can assume that she is in agreement with Law on this point.

In 'Cursory Thoughts' Cockburn turns to the further question whether God or a first cause exists necessarily (RSW 91–5) and distances herself from Law's criticism of Samuel Clarke's conception of necessary existence.[52] Before she engages properly with the question, she dismisses an objection that Law has raised against the view that God exists necessarily. Law worries that it is hard to conceive 'how *absolute Necessity* is reconcileable with *absolute Freedom*' (1732 [1731]: Note 10, 52). His concern is that if God is said to exist necessarily, then this would undermine God's freedom or, as Law puts it, 'take away that Freedom of Determination, that entire *Liberty of Indifference*, which our Author [i.e. William King] has sufficiently proved, to be a property of *God* himself, as well as *Man*' (Law 1732 [1731]: Note 10, 53).[53] Cockburn rejects that there is a conflict, because, as she points out, 'necessitated to *exist*, and necessitated to *act*, are very different ideas, and seem no way consequent one of the other' (RSW 92). She argues that this applies also to human beings: the fact that humans have been determined to exist by God's will does not entail that they lack 'perfect liberty, or freedom of choice' (RSW 92). More generally, her claim is that it does not follow from the fact that some being exists necessarily that the actions of this being are necessitated.

On this basis, Cockburn turns to 'the question itself, whether the divine being exists by an *absolute necessity*, or without any cause, ground, or reason of his existence' (RSW 92). This question rests on broader disputes concerning the Principle of Sufficient Reason ('PSR'), namely the principle that everything that exists has a cause or reason. Leibniz and Clarke, for instance, accept the PSR, while Law regards it as a 'false Maxim' (1732 [1731]: Remark e, 77). She prefaces her considerations by noting that it is far too difficult to settle the dispute. Rather than taking a clear stance on the issue, her aim is to reflect on the plausibility of the two options, namely, first, that God exists without a cause or reason, and, second, that God exists necessarily.

With regard to the former option, Cockburn asks whether it is possible that 'the first cause' could 'exist by mere chance' (RSW 92). If this was the case,

---

[52] See Law (1732 [1731]: Remark e, 74–8) and Clarke (1998 [1705]). For helpful further discussion, see Lascano (2019: 34–8).

[53] Quoted in part and paraphrased in Cockburn, RSW 92.

then 'it might possibly never have existed' (RSW 92). Furthermore, if the first cause existed without a reason, it could come and go out of existence without a reason and 'cease to exist in any time to come' (RSW 92). Cockburn worries further that if God exists without a reason or ground, then it would be difficult to find out whether other things exist necessarily or without a reason (RSW 93). Overall, denying God's necessary existence leads to many arbitrary contingencies, which makes this a rather unsatisfying option in Cockburn's view.

By contrast, Cockburn regards the other option, namely that God exists necessarily, as more plausible:

> On the other hand, *necessary existence* seems to give the mind something more satisfactory to rest on: if the first cause is necessarily existent, it must have always existed, and cannot possibly cease to exist: And not only *eternity*, but several other attributes, are deducible from this principle, as *immensity, unity,* &c. whereas from existence without any cause or reason, nothing seems to be certainly deducible. (RSW 93)

It is worth noting that Cockburn acknowledges that this option is not without difficulties either. If we accept that there is a first cause, we can enquire about its cause or reason of existence. In response one can propose that *necessity* is the cause or reason why there is a first cause. However, this proposal only works if the first cause and its ground or reason, namely necessity, are coetaneous, meaning that they come into existence simultaneously (RSW 93). Although Cockburn does not intend to give a decisive answer to the question whether God exists necessarily, having considered the problems for both options, there is little reason to doubt that she considers the view that God exists necessarily as more convincing.

2.3.2 Space

Cockburn's discussion of space (RSW 95–105) advances and critically engages with debates between realists and anti-realists about space.[54] Cockburn mentions that some philosophers who argue for the real existence of space have identified space with extension (RSW 95). She is probably thinking about Descartes, who goes even further and identifies space with corporeal matter, since for Descartes extension is the principal attribute of corporeal matter.[55] Locke, whom Cockburn regards as another realist about space, rejects the identification of space with corporeal matter (RSW 95). In Locke's view material things are not just extended, but also solid.[56] Cockburn compares

---

[54] For helpful further discussion, see Thomas (2013, 2015, 2018). See also Broad (2002: 158–62).
[55] See Descartes, *Principles* II.10, AT VIIIA:45; CSM I:227.   [56] See Locke, *Essay* II.iv.

realist with anti-realist views about space such as the positions developed by Law (1732 [1731]) and Watts (1733), who both claim that space is not a real entity, but rather exists only as an idea in the mind. She favours the realist position that space exists and is a real entity.[57]

Cockburn aims to understand what may have prompted anti-realists such as Law and Watts to deny the existence of space (RSW 96). She conjectures that the most likely ground 'for denying the real existence of space, is, that we know not in what class of beings to place it' (RSW 96). In her view this is the reason why Watts – who considers various possible metaphysical constitutions of space – concludes that space is nothing. However, for Cockburn, not being able to find out what kind of being space is points to our own ignorance of the metaphysical constitution of space and is no sufficient reason for denying its existence (RSW 96). Watts examines whether space is a substance or a mode, and if it is 'a substance, whether spirit or body' (RSW 96).[58] Cockburn challenges Watts, by asking, 'But how are we assured, that this is an adequate division of being?' (RSW 96).

Cockburn's strategy is to draw attention to our limited understanding of the metaphysical constitution of things. For her it is conceivable that there are other types of substances than those that are commonly acknowledged. It may also be possible that there are entities other than substances or modes. Cockburn finds inspiration in a 'conjecture' that Pierre Bayle ascribes to Pierre Gassendi.[59] Following Gassendi, Cockburn claims that she sees 'no absurdity in supposing, that there may be other substances, than either spirits or bodies' (RSW 97). She then 'venture[s] to propose a consideration, which may perhaps serve to confirm his conjecture' (RSW 97). Her proposal is to bring together the possibility that space is neither a bodily nor thinking substance but rather some other type of substance with the hypothesis that there is a great chain of being, namely the view that all kinds of being are arranged on a gradual scale. She describes the great chain of being as follows:[60]

> there is such a gradual progress in nature, that the most perfect of an inferior species comes very near to the most imperfect of that, which is immediately above it: that the whole chasm in nature, from a plant to a man, is filled up by such a gentle and easy ascent, that the little transitions from one species to

---

[57] This makes it plausible to regard her as a substantivalist, as Thomas (2013) proposes. Thomas defines substantivalism as 'the thesis that space or spacetime is a concrete, irreducible being, to be listed on the contents of the universe as an entity in its own right' (2013: 195).

[58] See Watts (1733: Essay I).

[59] Bayle's comments on Gassendi's view are quoted in Law (1732 [1731]: Note 6, 28–9).

[60] Cockburn does not invent the great chain of being thesis and mentions that it has been 'beautifully described by Mr. *Addison* and Mr. *Locke*' (RSW 97). See Locke, *Essay* III.vi.12. For further discussion of the great chain of being thesis, see Lovejoy (1936).

another are almost insensible: That if the scale of beings rises by such a regular progress so high as man, we may, by a parity of reason, suppose, that it still proceeds gradually through those beings, that are of a superior nature to him; that there is no manner of chasm left, no link deficient in this great chain of beings. (RSW 97)

According to the hypothesis that there is a great chain of being, there is no significant gap between one kind of being and the next. Cockburn observes that there is 'a gap between *senseless material*, and *intelligent immaterial* substance' (RSW 97), or – as she also puts it – a 'vast chasm betwixt body and spirit' (RSW 97). This leads her to ask what kind of being could fill this gap, assuming the great chain of being thesis is correct. Her proposal is that space may 'be such a being' (RSW 97) and can be defined as '*an immaterial unintelligent substance, the place of bodies, and of spirits, having some of the properties of both*' (RSW 97). Her thinking is that space would share the property of being unintelligent or senseless with bodies or material substances, and the property of being immaterial with immaterial thinking substances. By sharing properties of both it fills the gap between them.

Cockburn's proposal leaves open whether she focuses on finite or infinite intelligent immaterial substances or spirits. Neither option is straightforward. Let us consider the first option, namely that her proposal is to locate space on the great chain of being between senseless material bodies and finite intelligent immaterial substances. There are at least two worries that one could raise about this proposal. First, there is the question of whether space is finite. As Cockburn notes, many realists about space take for granted that space is infinite (RSW 104). If space is infinite, then it is not clear why an infinite being would be placed between finite bodies and finite immaterial thinking substances. However, Cockburn is not as confident as many of her contemporaries that space is infinite. In her view, not knowing what the boundaries of space are is no reason to infer that space is infinite, but rather only reveals how narrow our understanding is (RSW 104–5). Another worry concerns Cockburn's agnosticism about the metaphysical constitution of the human mind. As we have seen in Section 2.2.3, Cockburn accepts that it is possible that material beings have the power to think. It is worth noting that it does not follow from this that all thinking substances would be material. Cockburn follows Locke and maintains that God is an immaterial thinking substance (RSW 103). The point is that she admits that it is possible that finite thinking substances are material and this raises the question as to why she assumes, in her discussion of the great chain of being, that spirits or thinking substances are immaterial. If instead there are finite material thinking substances, then the initial attraction of her proposal is lost, because either space would have to be placed between unthinking material substances and thinking material substances – which are both material substances – or between material thinking substances and immaterial thinking substances, which are both thinking substances.

Let us turn to the other option, namely that her proposal is to place space between unintelligent material substances and an infinite intelligent immaterial substance.[61] In Cockburn's view, there is one infinite intelligent immaterial substance and that is God. Although this option avoids the problems that I raised for the first option, it is not without problems either. Given this option, one can ask where finite human beings, who consist of mind and body, can be placed on the scale: are they to be placed below or above space? They have material bodies, which brings them closer to unthinking material bodies than space that is said to be immaterial. However, they are also intelligent – a property that they share with God but not with space. Consequently, it is not clear whether human beings would be placed below or above space, and this may undermine the hypothesis that there is a great chain of being.

Unfortunately, Cockburn does not say enough about these puzzles and I do not want to speculate any further what she might have said in response to these puzzles. Overall, I am less confident than Thomas (2013, 2015) that Cockburn accepts the great chain of being thesis and endorses the account of space that she develops in 'Cursory Thoughts'. In my view, it is important to take seriously that she repeatedly emphasizes how limited our understanding of metaphysics is. Nevertheless, she deserves credit for highlighting that there can be other types of substances or other kinds of beings than those that have been traditionally included among the entities that compose the universe. Furthermore, her proposal that space could be a further type of substance that shares some properties with one type of substance and other properties with another type of substance is certainly original.

3 Moral Philosophy

Cockburn engages with moral questions in many of her writings. The aim of this section is to examine core themes of her moral philosophy. Cockburn draws a distinction between questions concerning the 'first ground' or the foundation of morality and questions concerning the practice of morality. Section 3.1 focuses on the former, namely her metaphysics of morality, and examines her account of human nature and how moral fitnesses arise from human nature, and further asks whether Cockburn can be said to endorse a version of moral naturalism. Section 3.2 turns to her views on moral practice and pays special

---

[61] Although Thomas (2013: 209–10) does not explicitly address the two different interpretive options that I draw attention to, she seems to interpret Cockburn in terms of this second option.

attention to her account of moral motivation. It considers three principles that she regards as motivationally important, namely the fitnesseses of things, conscience or the moral sense, and the will of God. Section 3.3 examines in what sense Cockburn may be said to be an intellectualist and how she challenges theological voluntarism. Section 3.4 discusses Cockburn's contributions to debates concerning self-interest, self-love, and benevolence in eighteenth-century British moral philosophy.

3.1 Moral Metaphysics

3.1.1 Human Nature

Cockburn argues throughout her philosophical writings that human nature is the foundation or 'ground' of morality.[62] She regards a human being as 'a *rational* and *social* as well as *sensible* being' (RSW 119). This statement provides a pointed summary of her account of human nature. For Cockburn, sensibility, rationality, and sociability are all important components of human nature, and she argues that neglecting any one of these components will lead to 'a partial consideration of human nature' (RSW 130).[63]

It is worth examining more closely how she understands sensibility, rationality, and sociability and what role each of these components plays in her moral philosophy. As sensible beings, humans seek pleasure and try to avoid pain (RSW 119). Sensibility is only one component of human nature and plays a subordinate role, as becomes clear in comparisons that Cockburn draws between humans and non-human animals. Humans share the capacity to feel pleasure or pain with non-human animals, but they differ from them insofar as they are also rational beings. Indeed, Cockburn goes so far as to argue that 'as reasonable beings, we are manifestly superior to them' (RR 184).[64] On the basis of this superiority and the differences between the natures of humans and non-human animals, she argues, it can be 'fit and reasonable to treat [animals] in *another manner*, than would be fit from any of us to our fellow-creatures' (RR 184). For Cockburn this entails that it is acceptable for humans to use animals as food for self-preservation, though she also makes clear that animals should not have to suffer any unnecessary pain (RR 184–5). Insofar as humans are rational beings, we have the mental capacities that enable us to make rational choices

---

[62] See Cockburn, *Defence* 43–7, RSW 107, 114–15, 119, 124–5, 127–8, 130, RR 184–6, 195, 205–10.

[63] For helpful further discussion of how human nature plays an important role in Cockburn's moral philosophy, see Bolton (1993), Green (2015), Sheridan (2007, 2018a). Her account of human nature is also discussed in De Tommaso (2017) and Sheridan (2018b), but these papers focus only on sociability and rationality.

[64] See also Cockburn, RR 211–14.

and 'ought to act suitably to the reason and nature of things' (RSW 119). According to Cockburn, humans are by nature not only sensible and rational beings but also social beings. As social beings, it is natural for us to desire and promote the good of others (RSW 119). For instance, Cockburn argues that it is natural for a mother to show parental affection and be concerned for her child and that this benevolent tendency cannot be reduced to self-interest (RSW 124–5).[65]

Cockburn does not merely describe the three components of human nature, namely sensibility, rationality, and sociability, but she also maintains that we can derive *moral obligations* from the fact that humans have specific natures.[66] More precisely, she believes that it follows from the fact that humans are by nature sensible, rational, and social beings that they ought to act suitably or fittingly to their nature. One may wonder why the fact that humans have certain natures establishes a moral obligation to act in accordance with one's nature. Cockburn responds to such worries as follows:

> To ask, why a rational being should choose to act according to reason, or why a social being should desire the good of others, is full as absurd, as to ask why a sensible being should choose pleasure rather than pain. If such a question is to be answered, the answer will be the same in either case, these ends are to be chosen, because suitable to the nature of beings with such and such capacities. (RSW 119)

As stated here, Cockburn believes that creatures with a certain nature ought to act in ways that are 'suitable' to this nature. The passage intimates further that human beings have been created with the purpose to make best use of their nature.[67] Thus, Cockburn believes that humans insofar as they are sensible ought to seek pleasure and avoid pain, but that as rational beings they additionally have an obligation to act rationally and as social beings they ought 'to promote the good of others' (RSW 119).

Cockburn argues not only that sensibility is merely one component of human nature, but she also distinguishes different kinds of happiness and claims that happiness does not merely consist in sensible pleasure.[68] Although she is willing to acknowledge that insofar as we are sensible beings '*sensible good* ... may make a considerable *part* of our happiness' (RR 205), she emphasizes that there is also 'some different kind of happiness' (RR 205),

---

[65] See also Cockburn, RR 159, and Correspondence 237.

[66] For further details concerning Cockburn's account of moral obligation, see RSW 119, 140–6, RR 170–1, 178–80, and her correspondence with Sharp, in *Works* 2:353–460.

[67] Cockburn also expresses teleological views in other parts of her writings. For instance, see RR 208–13. See also Sheridan (2007, 2018a).

[68] See Cockburn, RSW 119, 131, RR 205–6.

which is available to us 'as *reasonable* beings' (RR 205). For Cockburn reason is superior to the senses and thus the pleasure that we can receive by means of the senses does not provide the same type of satisfaction as the good that is '*proper*' to 'our superior faculties' (RR 205). She proposes that this proper good can be found in '*truth and virtue*' (RR 205) and lead to the happiness of rational beings.

It is worth examining further why Cockburn regards sociability as important in addition to sensibility and rationality. Let us imagine a scenario where someone faces a choice between either helping a family member or helping a stranger – and so is unable to help both. It will not be sufficient to rely on rationality alone for making a choice, because one could do as much good by helping a stranger as a family member. If we take seriously that humans are not just rational beings, but also social creatures, then it is clear, Cockburn argues, that one will and should help one's family member. Her honest labourer example supports this point:

> Ask an honest labourer, why he wears himself out with toils and cares to provide for his family, to feed and clothe a parcel of troublesome children. Would he answer, that this action was fitted to do good, and to prevent harm? No, certainly, for he would easily see, that as much good might be done by taking care of some other family: but he would readily answer, that truly he thought it behoved him to take care of his own; that his wife and children were very dear to him; and who should take care of them, if he did not? (RR 152)

In the immediately following passage Cockburn contrasts the honest labourer example with the example of 'a jolly neighbour' who spends all his money drinking and playing in the pub and fails to take care of his family:

> Tell him again of a jolly neighbour, who enjoys himself at the ale-house, drinking and playing away all he can get, whilst his family is left to go naked and starve; would he not instantly cry out, What an unnatural wretch is that! The very beasts take care of their young! These are the most natural senti-ments of a well disposed, though uncultivated mind; and they arise directly from the relations and fitness of things, and a disinterested benevolence, which guide him to virtuous practice, tho' he never heard of any of those terms. And that most perfect rule of life, *To do unto all men, as we would they should do unto me*, which is the sum of all the social virtues, is plainly deduced from the natural relation of equality we bear to each other, and a fitness resulting from thence: yet nothing is more easy and intelligible to common capacities. (RR 152)

These examples suggest that it is natural for us to be affected by the good and wellbeing of others. However, one may worry that there is a tension between her claim about equality and her view that it is appropriate to prioritize helping family members over strangers. The question of whether it is appropriate to be partial towards family members or close friends is pressing, because one could also be social without being partial.[69] To address this worry, I believe that it is helpful to turn to Cockburn's remarks on how human beings are part of 'a system of creatures' (RSW 114) or part of 'a system of social beings' (RR 149, 216). As these expressions suggest, she regards humans as part of a larger whole and believes that they are 'designed to promote each other's welfare' (RR 149). She writes:

> Mankind is a system of creatures, that continually need one another's assistance, without which they could not long subsist. It is therefore necessary, that everyone, according to his capacity and station, should contribute his part towards the good and preservation of the whole, and avoid whatever may be detrimental to it. For this end they are made capable of acquiring social or benevolent affections, (probably have the seeds of them implanted in their nature) with a moral sense or conscience, that approves of virtuous actions, and disapproves the contrary. (RSW 114)

Cockburn's view that human beings are part of a larger system and interconnected with their fellow human beings provides further insight into her claims about human sociability. On the one hand, it shows how humans depend on each other and how the happiness of individuals is related to everyone else's happiness. On the other hand, Cockburn acknowledges that due to varying and limited abilities and capacities each individual can only 'contribute his part towards the good and preservation of the whole' (RSW 114) but is not in a position to promote everyone's good. On this basis, it becomes plausible for individuals to prioritize promoting the good of others who are near and close to them, such as family members. If each individual focuses on supporting those who are closely related to them within the 'system of social beings', then (under ideal circumstances) it will be likely that everyone can count on social support within their close social circle, which in turn would be good for the whole of humankind. Alternatively, if one decides whether to help a family member or a stranger, say, by tossing a coin, then the risk of moral luck will increase and it will be more randomn whether individuals will be able to receive the help of others. Hence, Cockburn's philosophy – and her views concerning the 'system of social creatures' in particular – provides resources for explaining that sociability can be reconciled with partiality towards family members or close friends.

As we have seen, Cockburn emphasizes that humans are social beings. Yet one may wonder whether sociability is an additional component of human

---

[69] I thank Xiao Qi and Enrico Galvagni for helpful discussion of these issues.

nature besides sensibility and rationality or whether sociability can be explained in terms of sensibility and rationality and, if so, reduced to them.[70] To address this question, we have to examine more closely how Cockburn understands sensibility and sociability respectively. In passages where she considers sensibility, she tends to associate sensibility with pleasure and pain.[71] Moreover, she observes that sensible beings are 'liable to many external accidents, to pains and sufferings' (RSW 130), calls the good that sensible beings choose 'natural or sensible good' (RSW 119),[72] and acknowledges that if our focus is turned to our sensible nature, 'the relation of things to our own happiness ... is a very material relation' (RSW 120). This suggests that sensibility in Cockburn's philosophical writings concerns the feeling of pleasure and pain that is caused by external material objects. By contrast, when she considers sociability, she speaks of 'benevolent' or 'social affections' (RSW 113–14, 123–4, RR 167), as well as 'public affections' (RR 158) or 'disinterested affections' (RSW 123, RR 164–5, 167). This makes it plausible that she distinguishes the mental capacity to feel sensations or to feel pleasure and pain from the mental capacity to have benevolent or social affections. If this is correct, then sensibility and sociability would each be related to different mental capacities and this would help explain why sociability cannot be reduced to sensibility.[73]

Yet the question remains whether sociability can be reduced to rationality or a combination of rationality and sensibility. Cockburn does not explicitly address this concern, but given that she understands sociability in affective terms, it is unlikely that she would accept that sociability can be reduced to rationality alone. Moreover, if it is correct, as suggested above, that for her sensibility concerns feelings of pleasure and pain, then it is not clear how a combination of rationality and sensibility could sufficiently explain the affective aspect of sociability. This makes it more likely that for Cockburn sociability is a further component of her account of human nature in addition to rationality and sensibility.

So far I have argued that Cockburn regards sensibility, rationality, and sociability as important components of human nature. She emphasizes that a human being is 'a *compound* creature' (RR 206) and distances her view both from the view of the Stoics, who regard humans as rational and social beings but neglect sensibility, and from views held by critics of Stoic philosophy who regard humans as merely sensible beings but neglect their rational and

---

[70] I thank Dominik Perler for prompting me to think more about this issue.

[71] For instance, see Cockburn, RSW 119, 130–1, RR 181, 184–6, 188, 213.

[72] See also Cockburn RR 205.

[73] See RR 161–3 for further textual evidence that Cockburn distinguishes sensations from other mental capacities.

social nature (RSW 130, RR 205–6). The mistake of both, she claims, lies 'in a *partial* consideration of human nature' (RSW130). Cockburn is less confident than the Stoics that happiness is fully attainable in this life, but she believes that had the Stoics taken our sensible nature more seriously, and especially our exposure to pain and suffering, this 'might have led them to the knowledge of a future state' (RSW 130). Cockburn believes that it is important to acknowledge that many are advantaged or disadvantaged on external and contingent grounds in this life and believes that such disadvantages will be overcome in the afterlife. This leads her to challenge the Stoic view that everyone can attain virtue in this life. By assuming that virtue can be attained through self-mastery and that goodness is intrinsic to virtue, the Stoics failed to give adequate consideration to external advantages and disadvantages. As a result, Cockburn claims, 'they were forced into the absurdities of maintaining, that *pain is no evil*' (RSW 130). By contrast, for her there is no question that pain is evil, and she believes that unjust disadvantages will be corrected in a future state (RSW 130–1, RR 205–6, *Works* 2:131).

Cockburn's moral philosophy is sometimes portrayed as having affinities with Stoic philosophy or being influenced by Stoicism.[74] Cockburn shares the Stoic ideal of following nature and there is good evidence that she was familiar with Stoic sources, but – as we have just seen – her engagement with Stoic philosophy was critical. She believes that they have not accurately identified all components of human nature. Thus Cockburn defends and prefers her own view that humans are by nature sensible, rational, and social beings.

3.1.2 Moral Fitnesses

Having outlined Cockburn's account of human nature, it is time to consider how it relates to her claims concerning moral fitnesses. The language of fitnesses and unfitnesses is particularly prominent in her late works on moral philosophy, namely *Remarks upon Some Writers* (1743) and *Remarks upon the Principles and Reasonings of Dr. Rutherforth's* Essay (1747), and several interpreters have characterized Cockburn's moral theory as a fitness theory.[75] In a footnote added to the reprinted version of *Defence*, which appeared as part of her *Works* in 1751, Cockburn addresses an objection by her contemporaries that her early work *Defence* is inconsistent with her later works on moral philosophy (*Defence* 46–7 n.).[76] She denies this charge in the footnote and claims 'that there is no real

---

[74] See Nuovo (2011: 248–50, 254–8, 261–3), Sheridan (2018a: 250–2; 2018b).

[75] See Green (2015), Sheridan (2007), Sund (2013), Thomas (2017).

[76] Although Bolton (1993: 570) and Sheridan (2007: 149 n. 6) have pointed out that it is unclear whether Cockburn or Thomas Birch, who edited her *Works*, is the author of the footnote, Sund

difference' (*Defence* 46 n.). In the note, she states that 'new terms have been since introduced into these subjects; we talk now of essential differences, nature, relation, truth, and fitness of things: but the meaning is the very same; for all these are to be sought in the nature of God, or of man' (*Defence* 46–7 n.). While Cockburn acknowledges that she introduced 'new terms' in her later works, she believes that her overall position has not changed. Given this new terminology, it is worth examining more closely how exactly fitnesses of things relate to her account of human nature. Can these terms be used interchangeably? Or is human nature more fundamental than the fitnesses of things, or vice versa?

I believe that we have textual evidence intimating that she regards human nature as more fundamental than the fitnesses of things. In *Remarks upon Some Writers*, Cockburn claims that fitnesses and unfitnesses 'result' from the natures of the beings that God 'is determined to create' (RSW 108):[77]

> Whether God will bring into actual existence a particular system of beings, of any determinate nature, depends undeniably on his sole will and pleasure; but whether that system of beings shall have such and such relations, from whence certain fitnesses and unfitnesses must result, depends not on his will, but on the nature of the beings he is determined to create. To suppose, that he may will them to have other relations, & c. is to suppose, that he may will them to be another kind of beings than he determined to create; for if they are the same, the relations and fitnesses resulting from their nature, are necessary and immutable. (RSW 107–8)

This passage suggests that there are three elements built into the view she describes here: first, there are the natures of things, second, there are relations, and, third, there are fitnesses and unfitnesses. For Cockburn each kind of being has a 'determinate nature'. Different kinds of beings form 'a system of beings' and the various beings of the system stand in relations to each other. She further argues that certain fitnesses and unfitnesses result from the relations that pertain in the system of beings. This intimates that Cockburn accepts that the natures of the kinds of beings in the system of beings have an ontologically fundamental status.[78] The relations that arise from the system of beings can be said to ontologically depend on the natures of things and the fitnesses and unfitnesses

---

(2013: 1–2, 32–3, 174) has established that it is written in Cockburn's hand. For further discussion, see also Green (2019).

[77] See also Cockburn, RSW 110.

[78] Of course, one can further ask how a system of beings itself comes into existence, and it can be argued that God who is the creator of a system of beings has to exist prior to the system of beings that he creates. Indeed, in the quoted passage above, Cockburn is willing to accept that God's will plays a role in the creation of a system of being. I am putting questions of how a system of beings is chosen or comes into existence aside here and am only making a claim about a system of beings that has already been chosen or come into existence.

depend again on the relations that exist among the natures of things. This means that the relations cannot be different from what they are unless the natures of things are also different, which would mean that there is another kind of being. One can give an account of the natures and relations in descriptive terms, but as soon as one turns to the fitnesses and unfitnesses that result from the natures and their relations normativity enters into Cockburn's view. To ask what is fit or unfit for a being with a certain nature is to ask what a being with such and such a nature ought or ought not to do.[79]

Cockburn further claims that the natures of things are eternal and immutable (RSW 107) and that the relations among these things are necessary (RSW 107). She also regards the relations and fitnesses that result from a system of beings as 'eternal and immutable' (RSW 110, 143). Let us consider what she means by this and in what sense natures, relations, and fitnesses can be said to be eternal and immutable. As Cockburn clarifies, when she speaks of the eternal and immutable nature of things, she does not make claims about particular individual beings such as Rachel or Ben, but rather she considers abstract general ideas that exist in the divine understanding (RSW 110, 144). This means that Cockburn's claim is not that particular individual beings such as Rachel, Ben, my neighbour's cat, or the cherry tree outside my window have existed eternally and will continue to do so, but rather her claim is that God has an abstract idea of all kinds of beings that he intends to create in his mind and once God has fixed on a particular system of beings that will become the actual world, these ideas cannot be changed any further. In this sense, they are immutable and exist eternally in God's mind. Once the natures of the kinds of beings that are part of a system of beings have been fixed, it is also fixed what relations follow from the natures of the kinds of beings. In this sense the relations can be said to be necessary. Moreover, Cockburn's claims about the necessity of fitnesses or unfitnesses are best understood in terms of normative necessity. According to Patricia Sheridan, 'Cockburn means to imply … that the fitnesses associated with human nature ought to be realized as a matter of *normative* necessity' (2018a: 250).

Several interpreters have noted that Cockburn's account of moral fitnesses is similar to Samuel Clarke's moral theory.[80] Some interpreters go even further and claim that Cockburn adopts Clarke's moral views or has learned the moral position that she puts forward from Clarke. Against such interpretations, Martha Brandt Bolton (1993) argues convincingly that Cockburn cannot have learned her moral view from Clarke, because she already held it at the time when she wrote her *Defence* in 1701–2 and Clarke did not deliver his second set of Boyle

---

[79] See Cockburn, RR 170–1.   [80] See Clarke (1711 [1706]) for details of his moral philosophy.

lectures, which includes his account of moral fitnesses, until 1705. Bolton's point is 'not that Trotter invented the moral theory she shared with Clarke', but rather that '[Trotter] didn't *learn* it from him' (Bolton 1993: 576).

3.1.3 Moral Naturalism

So far we have taken a close look at Cockburn's account of human nature and the relations and fitnesses that follow from it. However, one may wonder whether it is possible to further characterize her moral theory and what might be said about her view from a meta-ethical perspective. Here I want to focus on the question of whether she endorses a version of moral naturalism, since this question has received particular attention in the scholarly literature.[81] Cockburn's view that human nature is the ground or foundation of morality leads Patricia Sheridan to argue that Cockburn offers an 'anthropocentric view of morality' (2007: 141, 142; 2018a: 249). Moreover, Sheridan ascribes 'a version of moral naturalism' (2018a: 248) to Cockburn. According to Sheridan, Cockburn's version of moral naturalism 'encompasses both natural teleology and the eudaemonistic emphasis of traditional virtue ethics' (2018a: 248). Since Cockburn emphasizes the importance of acting in accordance with nature, Sheridan argues further that Cockburn's version of moral naturalism can be described as 'the view that "virtue consists in following nature"'(2018a: 248),[82] and she regards it as a 'kind of Stoic naturalism' (2018a: 251). As Sheridan specifies, for the Stoics following nature does not mean that one follows every natural impulse, but rather that one under the guidance of reason identifies the most appropriate way to live. For the Stoics, 'the end or goal of a human life is self-realization, or the perfection of human nature' (Sheridan 2018a: 251).

Sheridan contrasts Cockburn's version of naturalism with a reductivist version of moral naturalism. A reductivist moral naturalist believes that 'facts of morality are ultimately explicable with reference to non-moral facts about human psychology and physiology' (Sheridan 2018a: 252). Sheridan focuses on reductivist views that were held by Cockburn's predecessors and contemporaries during the early modern period such as the moral views developed by Thomas Hobbes and Bernard Mandeville. Sheridan describes the reductivist view as follows:

> On the reductivist view, the raw materials upon which morality works are
> egoistic impulses – desires and aversions – which must be regulated in order

---

[81] See Broad (2021), Green (2015), Sheridan (2007, 2018a).

[82] Sheridan here quotes Millar (1988), who calls the view 'that virtue consists in following nature' the 'Follow Nature doctrine' (1988: 165).

to be turned to good effect. A Hobbesian reductivist suggests that reason has a role to play in this, since it is reason that counsels general principles which, when observed, lead to the kinds of social accommodations most apt to satisfy our impulses. However, on the reductivist view, it is not such accommodations on their own, but, rather, the institutions of positive law, that confer obligatory force on the principles and mechanisms of communal morality. (Sheridan 2018a: 256–7)

Sheridan draws attention to a further difference between Cockburn's position and the views held by reductivist thinkers such as Hobbes or Mandeville. On their view, 'humans have no intrinsically moral motivations, nor does nature afford any objective basis for moral guidance' (Sheridan 2018a: 252). This is not to deny that reason can play an instrumental role in 'establishing principles and rules aimed at maximizing the satisfaction of egoistic aims, [but] these aims are amoral' (Sheridan 2018a: 252). On this reductivist view the natural impulses are amoral and morality can be seen as an additional layer that emerges in the context of civil society when positive institutions are created. According to Sheridan, 'this stands in sharp contrast to Cockburn's view of the relationship between nature and morality, according to which human nature itself provides an intrinsic moral standard of conduct, and does so independently of the institutions of civil society' (2018a: 252).

Having outlined Sheridan's interpretation of Cockburn's moral naturalism, it is worth pausing for a moment to reflect on the different philosophical issues that are built into her interpretation. First, there is the question of how moral naturalism is best understood. There are a variety of ways to be a moral naturalist.[83] As we have seen, Sheridan proposes that Cockburn's moral theory is naturalist insofar as she adopts the view that humans ought to live in accordance with nature. However, one can ask why Sheridan contrasts the following nature naturalism that she ascribes to Cockburn with another version of naturalism, namely reductivist naturalism. This question arises, because there are other possible contrast classes. One can argue that it is more obvious to contrast moral naturalism, understood in terms of following nature, with the view that morality (at least sometimes) requires acting against nature. Although Cockburn does not hold this view, others may argue that humans are by nature self-interested. If this is the case, and if one further accepts that self-interest is amoral, then in order to be moral one may have to act against one's self-interested nature.

Reductivist moral naturalism is the other version of naturalism that Sheridan considers. This view draws on more recent debates in meta-ethics. In meta-ethics it is common to ask whether there are objective moral facts that are

---

[83] For instance, see Miller (2003).

independent of human opinion. Those who affirm that there are such moral facts can be called moral realists. Next, one can enquire whether the moral facts are natural facts. Anyone who endorses the view that moral facts are natural can be said to be a moral naturalist. Now one can further ask whether natural moral facts can be reduced to other non-moral natural facts. Those who affirm that moral facts are reducible to non-moral natural facts are reductionists, or reductivists; those who deny this are non-reductionists.[84]

Sheridan owes us more detailed arguments as to why she focuses merely on the contrast she draws and does not consider other possible contrast classes. The fact that Cockburn rejects moral egoism held by thinkers such as Hobbes or Mandeville is not sufficient to decide whether her own moral view can be understood as a reductionist or non-reductionist version of moral naturalism. More generally, if we take seriously these other contrast classes, it is not any longer clear whether moral naturalism, understood in terms of following nature, and reductionist or reductivist moral naturalism are mutually exclusive views. If one wants to situate Cockburn's moral philosophy within meta-ethical frameworks, more consideration needs to be given to the question of whether Cockburn holds a reductionist or non-reductionist view. This requires closer examination as to whether the facts about human nature that Cockburn describes – namely that humans are sensible, rational, and social beings – are first of all natural non-moral facts, as a reductionist would argue, or whether they are inherently moral and non-reducible to non-moral natural facts, as a non-reductionist would argue. In this context, it may also be worth taking into consideration a point that Karen Green has raised in a critical response to Sheridan's naturalist interpretation, namely that Cockburn's view 'is not deeply naturalist, since it depends for its cogency on the belief that there is a good God, who has determined that our nature should be to be ethical, social beings, and who will ensure that virtue will be rewarded with happiness, if not in this life, in a life to come' (Green 2015: 95).[85]

Overall, it is plausible to regard Cockburn as a moral realist, if moral realism is understood as the view that there are objective moral facts that are independent of human opinion. However, it is difficult to map Cockburn's position onto the various sub-categories of moral realism such as moral naturalism that are used in present-day meta-ethical debates, because present-day moral naturalists tend to offer secular views. For Cockburn moral facts are grounded in the natural world, or more precisely have their foundation in human nature, but her moral philosophy has another layer insofar as she also acknowledges that

---

[84] See Miller (2003: 8).   [85] Green's paper responds to Sheridan (2007).

abstract general ideas of the natures of things and the relations that follow from them exist in God's mind.

Here I want to draw attention to two further issues that are built into Sheridan's interpretation. The question of whether humans are by nature self-interested or benevolent beings was widely debated in eighteenth-century British moral philosophy. Cockburn distances herself from views held by Hobbes, Mandeville, and others who claim that humans are by nature self-interested beings. Instead she argues that humans are by nature social and benevolent beings. In this respect her view is similar to Shaftesbury's, Hutcheson's, and Butler's views, but she does not agree with all other aspects of their philosophical views. I will return to this debate in Section 3.4, where I examine Cockburn's contribution to questions concerning self-interest and benevolence in British moral philosophy.

As I have mentioned above, Sheridan further points out that for Cockburn moral motivation is intrinsic to human nature, while moral egoists like Hobbes or Mandeville need to appeal to a source of moral motivation that is extrinsic to human nature (Sheridan 2018a: 253). As will become apparent in Section 3.2, Cockburn's account of moral motivation is more complex. Although she accepts that understanding what our human nature is and what the fitnesses are that arise from it can in principle motivate to act morally, she also acknowledges that not everyone is sufficiently intrinsically motivated to carry out moral obligations and thus she believes that the will of God can provide a helpful additional external motivation. This is the topic to which I turn in the next section.

3.2 Moral Practice

So far we have examined Cockburn's account of human nature and the relations and fitnesses that result from it, which can be said to constitute her metaphysics of morality. Cockburn's moral philosophy, however, is not restricted to examining the 'first grounds' or foundation of morality, but rather she also engages with philosophical questions concerning the practice of morality. Indeed, she emphasizes that it is important to distinguish the foundation or 'first grounds' of morality from moral practice or 'the force of the law' (*Defence* 47). As far as moral practice is concerned, Cockburn pays special attention to the question of what motivates humans to act morally. She is aware that not all human beings are sufficiently motivated to act in accordance with the fitnesses of things, namely the moral obligations that arise from the constitution of human nature. Although reflection on human nature and the fitnesses that arise from it can motivate some human beings to act morally, Cockburn also acknowledges additional principles that help to strengthen moral motivation.

For Cockburn there are three principles that are all important with regard to moral motivation, or our 'obligation to Moral practise' (Correspondence 186) as she calls it. The three principles concern the fitnesses of things, conscience or the moral sense, and the will of God.[86] She expresses this view succinctly in a letter to Ann Arbuthnot, dated 8 September 1738:

> whilst our Modern Moralists have contended to establish Moral Virtue, some on the Moral Sense alone, some on the Essential difference and Relations of things, and some on the sole Will of God, they have all been deficient; for neither of these Principles are sufficient exclusive of the others but all three together make an immoveable foundation <for> and obligation to Moral practise, the Moral sense or Conscience, and the Essential difference of things, discovering to us what the will of our Maker is. (Correspondence 186)

Cockburn shares the view with William Warburton that conscience or the moral sense, fitness relations or the essential difference of things, and the will of God form a 'threefold cord' (RSW 109).[87] As Warburton explains in *Divine Legation* (1738), human beings have different tempers and characters and some are more influenced or guided by passions, and others by reason. This leads Warburton to argue that the strengths with which the three principles – namely the moral sense, the essential difference of things, and the will of God – operate on different humans and motivate them to act can vary. In his view 'the *Moral Sense*, would strongly operate on those, who by the exact Temperature and Balance of the Passions, were disengaged enough to feel the Delicacy and Grandeur of the Moral Sense' (Warburton 1738: 37), while '*the Essential Difference* founded in the natural Relations of Things, will have its Weight with the Speculative, the abstracted and profound Reasoners, and on all those who excel in the Knowledge of Mankind' (1738: 37). 'The *Will of God* ... takes in all the Consequences of Obedience' (1738: 37–8), which in Warburton's view makes it a suitable motivational principle for most human beings. Warburton emphasizes that it is significant that there are these three different principles, because this helps to make sure that everyone irrespective of 'Ranks, Constitution, and Education' (1738: 37) will be motivated to act morally by at least one of the principles.

Cockburn agrees with Warburton that all three principles are motivationally important, but they differ about the answer to the question which of the principles is more fundamental than the others. While Warburton argues that

---

[86] Sund (2013: ch. 3) discusses these three principles in detail and regards them as the basis of Cockburn's theory of moral obligation. My reading differs from Sund's interpretation insofar as I read Cockburn as making a claim about 'obligation to Moral practise' (Correspondence 186) rather than just obligation.

[87] Indeed, she adopts the expression 'threefold cord' from Warburton (1738: 38). See also Warburton's preface in Cockburn, RR 147–8.

'*Compliance with the Will of God* ... hath the highest degree of Merit' (1738: 38), for Cockburn the fitnesses of things have a more fundamental status insofar as they not only motivate, but also offer a foundation of morality. In her view, the other two principles offer additional helpful motivation to perform our moral duties, but these principles provide no foundation of morality.

On this basis, let us examine more closely how Cockburn understands each of the three principles – namely the fitnesses of things, conscience or the moral sense, and the will of God – and what role they play with regard to moral motivation.

3.2.1 Fitnesses of Things

Since I have already commented on Cockburn's understanding of fitnesses in Section 3.1.2 above, I will restrict the discussion here to the question of whether moral fitnesses can be intrinsically motivating. Relatedly, one may also ask whether something that is internal to human nature can be morally obligatory and motivating. To shed light on Cockburn's thinking, it can be helpful to turn to a problem that William Warburton raises in *Divine Legation* (1738) for moral views that explain moral obligation as internal to the moral agent, and then consider Cockburn's response to Warburton.[88]

Warburton believes that it is important that there is a distinction between a lawgiver and the being that is subject to laws or moral rules, or, as he puts it, between an 'obliger' and the subject that is being obliged. He considers it to be 'the highest of Absurdities' to make someone 'at once the Obliger and Obliged' (1738: 47). Warburton argues that if one person has a moral obligation towards another, then the other person acquires a right to the thing in question. However, if the obliger and the being obliged are identical, then it is easy to release oneself from the obligation, which undermines its obligatory nature. Thus, Warburton concludes, 'If therefore the Obliger and Obliged should be one and the same Person, all Obligation there must be void of course; or rather there would be no Obligation begun' (1738: 47).[89]

Cockburn disagrees and answers 'that, in the common acceptation of the word, obligation implies only a perception of some ground or reason, upon which it is founded, but not necessarily a superior will' (RSW 140). Her view is that by understanding what the natures of things are and the relations and fitnesses that follow from them, we can also grasp what moral obligations follow from them.[90] Let us consider how Cockburn might respond to Warburton's worry that if moral agents oblige themselves they can easily

---

[88] For further discussion of Cockburn's response to Warburton, see Broad (2021).
[89] See also Warburton's preface in Cockburn, RR 147–8.   [90] See Cockburn, RSW 140–2.

release themselves from the obligation. At this stage, it is important to take into consideration that moral obligations, according to Cockburn, are grounded in human nature or, as she also states, the nature of things. This means that human nature provides an objective foundation for moral obligations and moral agents cannot alter or release themselves from their moral obligations simply because they may not feel like carrying out their duty. Warburton's worry seems to assume that if there is no distinction between an obliger and the obliged then obligations cease to be binding. However, Cockburn's view avoids this problem, because her account of human nature provides an objective foundation of moral obligation.

Under ideal circumstances, understanding our moral obligations should also motivate us to act accordingly. However, Cockburn is aware that it would be naïve to assume most people would carry out their moral obligations simply because there are certain fitnesses from which they follow. This insight is reflected in her statement 'that the knowledge of the *essential difference of things* would not alone be generally effectual to influence a society of Atheists to the practice of virtue, I readily grant' (RSW 142). This makes it worth considering how, according to Cockburn, conscience and the will of God can offer additional motivation to carry out one's moral obligations, which is the topic of the next two sections.

3.2.2 Conscience or the Moral Sense

Cockburn acknowledges that conscience or the moral sense can influence the practice of morality and be motivationally relevant.[91] Before we turn to her own account of conscience, it can be helpful to comment for a moment on accounts of conscience or the moral sense held by her contemporaries that she rejects. Cockburn accepts that the terms 'conscience' and 'moral sense' can be used interchangeably, but she emphasizes that in her view conscience, or the moral sense, is not a 'blind instinct' (RSW 109, 116–17, RR 157, Correspondence 224, 242–3). She ascribes the view that the moral sense is a blind instinct to Francis Hutcheson (RR 157, Correspondence 242), though it is questionable whether Hutcheson himself would accept this characterization (Boeker 2022). He introduces the moral sense as a form of perception by means of which we approve or disapprove of morally good or bad actions (Hutcheson 2004 [1725], 2002 [1728]). His view was widely discussed among eighteenth-century British

---

[91] For further discussion of Cockburn's account of conscience, see Bolton (1993), De Tommaso (2017), Lustila (2020), Myers (2012), Sund (2013), Waithe (1987–95: 3:110–12). Bolton and Lustila engage with Cockburn's later works on moral philosophy RSW and RR but do not make explicit that conscience is one among three principles that together form a 'threefold cord' (RSW 109); Sund notes this point.

moral philosophers. Several of his eighteenth-century critics ascribe to Hutcheson the view that the moral sense is a blind instinct or regard the moral sense as an instinct.[92] We can assume that Cockburn's interpretation of Hutcheson is shaped by reading the works of his critics such as Gay, Johnson, Rutherforth, or Warburton – all authors of works that Cockburn critically discusses in her writings.

Cockburn rejects the view that the moral sense is a blind instinct, because she believes that there has to be some prior moral standard by means of which the moral sense approves or disapproves of certain actions. For her, conscience, or the moral sense, is an inner principle that leads us to assess our actions in light of a prior moral standard, namely our moral obligations. If we have transgressed our moral obligations, then as a result of our conscience we will stand 'self-condemned' (RSW 109). The important point for Cockburn is that moral obligations, or moral standards, must have already been established before conscience or the moral sense can operate and make us feel uneasy if we neglect them, as she states in the following passage:

> the uneasiness we feel upon the practice of anything contrary to what moral sense approves, is a *consequence* of the obligation, not the *foundation* of it, and only shows, that we are conscious of being obliged to certain actions, which we cannot neglect without standing self-condemned; self-condemnation manifestly presupposing some *obligation*, that we judge ourselves to have transgressed. (RSW 109)

Cockburn regards conscience as a helpful motivational principle that prompts us to act in accordance with moral obligations. However, it does not follow from this that humans are determined to act in accordance with conscience. As she makes clear in a letter to Arbuthnot from 8 September 1738, humans have 'the power . . . to act or not act as conscience directs' and this constitutes us as 'free Agents' (Correspondence 186).

3.2.3 Will of God

Although some people are motivated to carry out their moral obligations by acting in accordance with the fitnesses of things or by following their own conscience, Cockburn acknowledges that not all human beings are sufficiently motivated by these principles. She believes that the will of God and divine retributions in a future state can offer a helpful additional motivation to act morally (RSW 114–15). Indeed, Cockburn regards it as a matter of divine foresight that the will of God provides an additional and '*new motive*' (RSW 115). Otherwise, it would be more

---

[92] See Gay (1732 [1731]: xxxi–xxxiii), Johnson (1731: 29–30), Rutherforth (1744: ch. 5), Warburton (1738: 36).

likely 'that many would be drawn by irregular passions [and] deviate from the rule of their duty' (RSW 114). This in turn could disadvantage those who regularly adhered to their moral duty. To avoid that some would benefit from transgressing moral laws and others, who carry out their moral duty, suffer great disadvantages, God 'determined, agreeably to his goodness and rectitude, to make suitable retributions in a future state' (RSW 114). For Cockburn 'it is plain' that divine retributions in the afterlife introduce 'no *new moral obligation*, in the usual sense of that word' (RSW 114). Rather, the important point for her is that 'the very notion of reward and punishment implies an *antecedent* duty or obligation, the conforming or not conforming to which, is the only ground of reward and punishment' (RSW 114). She develops this point further in the following passage:

> When God was pleased to declare to the world this his determination, in making known to mankind more explicitly, that the law of their nature was likewise *the will* of their creator, he brought them indeed under an *add-itional* obligation to observe it, obedience to his will being one of the principal fitnesses resulting from the nature and relations of things. But in declaring, that he would eternally *reward or punish* those, who obeyed or disobeyed, he gave them only a new *motive* to the performance of their duty, but no new *foundation* of it: the rule, and reason, and obligation of virtue remained as before, in the immutable nature and necessary relations of things. (RSW 114–15)

To sum up, Cockburn believes that all three principles – namely the fitnesses of things, conscience or the moral sense, and the will of God – mutually support each other and are all motivationally important for the practice of morality.

3.3 Intellectualism and Voluntarism

So far we have seen that Cockburn defends the view that morality has a foundation that is independent of God's will and that we can acquire moral knowledge by reflecting on human nature and the relations and fitnesses that arise from it. This has prompted several interpreters to regard her as an intellectualist.[93] In the scholarly literature, intellectualism is distinguished from theological voluntarism. Roughly speaking, the issue of dispute is whether something is morally good because God commands it, as a voluntarist would say, or whether God commands something, because it is morally good, as an intellectualist would argue. Putting this differently, the question is whether God *wills* or *knows* what is morally good. Cockburn makes the claim that 'virtue therefore does not acquire its fitness from *command*: But God commanded it,

---

[93] See Bolton (1993), De Tommaso (2017), Green (2015, 2019), Kelley (2004), Thomas (2017).

because he saw, that it was absolutely right and fit, the indispensable duty of a rational and social being' (RSW 121); this suggests that she is an intellectualist. Cockburn critically responds to several eighteenth-century moral philosophers and theologians who defend voluntarist views. Let us now take a closer look at how and why Cockburn rejects voluntarist views and examine what alternative intellectualist position she favours.

First of all, Cockburn opposes any version of voluntarism that would make it possible for God to change by an arbitrary act of will what is good and evil such 'that *pleasure* can be *pain*, and *pain pleasure*' (*Defence* 43). In her own view, human nature is the foundation of morality and this rules out that God can, by an arbitrary act of will, change what is good or evil. However, she also acknowledges that many of her contemporaries do not share her view and instead explain the foundation of morality with appeal to rewards and punishments. For instance, the Remarker – a critic of Locke's *Essay* – claims that Locke seems 'to ground [his] Demonstration upon Future Punishments and Rewards, and upon the arbitrary Will of the Law giver' (*Second Remarks* 21). In the view of the Remarker, these are not 'the first Grounds of *Good and Evil, Vertue and Vice*' (*Second Remarks* 21). In response to the Remarker's voluntarist reading of Locke, Cockburn offers an intellectualist reading of Locke and accuses the Remarker of failing to distinguish between 'the *first grounds* of good and evil' and 'the force of the law' (*Defence* 47). According to Cockburn, 'Mr. *Locke* says, that the will of God, rewards and punishments, can only give morality the force of a law' (*Defence* 47), but, she adds, 'that does not make them the *first grounds* of good and evil' (*Defence* 47). In Cockburn's view God's will cannot arbitrarily change, but rather is constrained by the natures of things. Although it is not clear whether Locke would share Cockburn's intellectualist interpretation,[94] we can see that Cockburn's own moral philosophy offers resources for avoiding this version of voluntarism. Her view is that God's will and divine sanctions can serve as an additional motivation to act in accordance with moral obligations and thereby help enforce morality, but the foundation of morality does not presuppose God's will.

Even if we grant that God does not have arbitrary powers to change what is good and evil, Cockburn's opponents may be more concerned about other versions of voluntarism. Indeed, they may accept this point but instead draw attention to another more pressing issue, namely the question of whether an act of divine will is required during God's initial creation. Cockburn argues that human nature is the foundation of morality, but this raises the question of how human beings and their natures have been created. A critic of Cockburn's view

---

[94] For further discussion, see Green (2019), Randall Ward (1995), Tuckness (1999).

could argue that human nature depends on God's will, because humans and their natures would not exist had God not willed to create them.[95]

Cockburn addresses the worry that the initial creation of humans and their nature presupposes an act of divine will by emphasizing that it is important to distinguish between the divine will and the divine understanding (RSW 107, 122). In her view the divine understanding plays a role during God's initial creation of humans and other kinds of being and it cannot be solely explained in terms of acts of divine will. For her the natures of things and the relations that follow from them 'are eternally perceived by the divine understanding' (RSW 107). She regards them as abstract ideas in the divine understanding and makes clear that 'this depends not on a determination of the will of God' (RSW 107).

One of Cockburn's main targets in *Remarks upon Some Writers* is Edmund Law (1732 [1731]). Law would most likely not be satisfied with Cockburn's proposal to draw a distinction between the divine will and the divine understanding, since he anticipates such a rebuttal in his Notes on William King's *An Essay on the Origin of Evil* (Law 1732 [1731]: Note Q, 294–300). Law believes that shifting the focus towards the divine understanding is unconvincing, because the further question remains how God chooses one world, which becomes the actual world, from the many possible worlds that he could create. Contrary to Leibniz, who claims that there is a best possible world, Law argues that there is no best possible world among the many possible worlds that God could create. In support of this position, Law points out that any of the possible worlds could have been better: first, by creating more individuals, second, by adding other varieties of creatures, or, third, by giving created beings more and stronger appetites (Law 1732 [1731]: Note Q, 297). However, as Law also notes, there is no guarantee that any of the options that could make a world better would result in a better world, since each option comes with the risk of increasing evil. This leads Law to infer that God cannot be guided by his understanding when he decides which of the many possible worlds to make actual, but arbitrarily chooses one world by an act of divine will.[96]

Cockburn concedes that Law's argument shows that there is no best possible world among the many worlds that God could create. Even if 'God is indeed perfectly free to choose, which of them he will bring into actual existence' (RSW, 110), Cockburn believes that this does not undermine moral fitness theory. She criticizes Law for mingling two philosophical debates together, namely, first, whether there are fitnesses of things independent of a divine will, and, second, whether there is a best possible world. In her view, these two

---

[95] Cockburn addresses such worries in *Defence* 43–4, RSW 107–8, 121–2, 143–4.

[96] See Law (1732 [1731]: Note Q, 296–9, Note 53, 301–14). For further discussion, see Thomas (2017).

debates do not depend on each other and should be kept separate and 'the defenders of this antecedent fitness, have no need of supposing, that the present system is *absolutely best*' (RSW 110). Irrespective of whether there are possible worlds that are better than the actual world, Cockburn argues that the beings of each possible world form a system that produces 'different relations, and fitnesses resulting from them' (RSW 110) and that 'the relations of all *possible* systems must be eternally in the divine *mind* ... they cannot therefore be dependent on *will*' (RSW 110). Again, we see that Cockburn shifts the focus from the divine will towards the divine understanding and argues that the divine understanding plays a more important role than her voluntarist opponents acknowledge.

One advantage of Cockburn's position in comparison with the views held by voluntarists of her day is that every human being can acquire moral knowledge without revelation and without a teacher or guide.[97]

3.4 Self-interest, Self-love, and Benevolence

Cockburn actively contributes to lively debates in eighteenth-century British moral philosophy on whether actions that focus on the good of others, such as helping a friend or a stranger in need, have their origin in self-interest or in some natural tendency towards benevolence that is inherent to our human constitution. As she makes explicit in a letter to Arbuthnot, dated 2 October 1747, for her the issue of dispute 'is not how much or how little disinterested benevolence is practised in the world, but whether that which there is of it, proceeds from an artificial *association* of Ideas, or from a disposition to delight in the good of others *implanted in the nature of man*' (Correspondence 236–7). This means that Cockburn is primarily interested in understanding what the origin of benevolent actions is. To shed further light on her position, it is helpful to situate her view within the context of the debates concerning self-interest and benevolence in eighteenth-century British moral philosophy.

The view that humans are by nature self-interested or selfish beings – as defended, for instance, by Thomas Hobbes (1994 [1651]) or Bernard Mandeville (1723 [1714]) – has prompted a number of critical responses and attempts to show that humans are not merely self-interested beings, but also by nature benevolent.[98] One such attempt to push back against the thesis that humans are purely self-interested beings can be found in Francis Hutcheson's philosophy (2004 [1725], 2002 [1728]). Hutcheson believes that the perception

---

[97] See Section 4.1.2 for further discussion of these issues.
[98] For instance, see Shaftesbury (2001 [1711]), Hutcheson (2004 [1725], 2002 [1728]), Butler (2017). For further discussion, see Gill (2006), Maurer (2019).

of disinterested benevolence or moral goodness is of a different kind than the pleasure one receives from perceiving natural goodness such as perceiving a sunset or flowers in a field (Hutcheson 2004 [1725]: 89–90). This leads Hutcheson to argue that we have a distinct moral sense by means of which we 'perceive *Virtue*, or *Vice* in our selves, or others' (2002 [1728]: 17). According to him, all humans have been equipped with a moral sense and some other senses, in addition to the external five senses. Several of Hutcheson's contemporaries challenge his postulation of a moral and various other senses. One strategy, which a number of Hutcheson's critics adopt, is to accept the phenomenon of benevolent social interaction. More precisely, these critics accept that humans tend to be concerned about the happiness of others, but they appeal to the association of ideas to explain how benevolent actions can ultimately be traced back to self-interest.[99] Before I elaborate on how the association of ideas is meant to work, according to Hutcheson's critics Gay (1732 [1731]) and Johnson (1731), let me outline how Cockburn situates her position within these debates.

Cockburn is in agreement with Hutcheson's critics Gay, Johnson, and Rutherforth that it is problematic to appeal to a moral sense, if a moral sense is understood as a blind instinct (RSW 116–7, RR 157).[100] However, she opposes their proposal that benevolent actions can ultimately be traced back to self-interest. Instead she is convinced that humans are by nature social and benevolent beings. This means that Cockburn is aiming to find a different explanation for the origin of human benevolence. She intends to develop a position that neither relies on a Hutchesonian moral sense nor appeals to associations of ideas or other sophisticated explanations that ultimately reduce benevolent actions to self-interest.

To understand why Cockburn rejects appeals to associations of ideas that aim to show that benevolent actions have their origin in self-interest, it is worth taking a closer look at how Gay and Johnson argue for the association of ideas and how Cockburn criticizes their views.[101] In his 'Preliminary Dissertation' Gay argues that benevolent actions can be explained in terms of reason and ultimately arise from self-interest or '*private Happiness*' (1732 [1731]: xxxii). He acknowledges that we do not always actively perceive our private happiness when we perform actions or interact with others, and

---

[99] See Gay (1732 [1731]), Johnson (1731).   [100] See also Section 3.2.2.

[101] Cockburn discusses Gay's 'Preliminary Dissertation' in RSW 106, 113. It is unlikely that Cockburn at the time of writing RSW was aware that Gay was the author, since 'Preliminary Dissertation' was published anonymously and prefixed to Law's edition of King's *Essay on the Origin of Evil*. Cockburn attributes 'Preliminary Dissertation' to Law, 'the author of the notes' (RSW 113). For further discussion of Cockburn's response to Gay, see Lustila (2020). Cockburn discusses Johnson's *Essay on Moral Obligation* in RSW 116–31.

believes that associations of ideas, which he also regards as habits, offer an explanation for this (Gay 1732 [1731]: xxxii, li–lvii).[102] According to Gay, we start to form associations in the following way: first of all, we perceive or imagine how certain things such as money are means towards our own happiness, which Gay understands in terms of self-interest. Then we start to 'annex Pleasure to those things' (Gay 1732 [1731]: liii). Over time the things that initially were merely means towards happiness become so closely associated with pleasure in our mind 'that one cannot present itself but the other will also occur' (Gay 1732 [1731]: liv). The example of money illustrates this process well. As Gay observes, many people have a strong desire for money and once they have realized how advantageous it is to have money they start to 'receive an actual Pleasure in obtaining it' (1732 [1731]: liv). Over time they cease to see that money is only an intermediate means to happiness and 'they join Money and Happiness immediately together, and content themselves with the phantastical Pleasure of having it' (Gay 1732 [1731]: liv). This leads them to pursue money as if it were 'a real *End*' (Gay 1732 [1731]: liv). According to Gay, the association between pleasure and money (or some other things) can continue even if we have forgotten why we initially started to associate pleasure with money (or another thing), or if there is no proper connection.

Thomas Johnson follows Gay in explaining human benevolence with appeal to the association of ideas, but he gives further consideration to the role of education:[103]

> At first a Man perceives, or is taught from his Infancy, that as he lives in a *social State*, so his Happiness is necessarily connected with that of other Men; that the Esteem of others is useful and necessary for him, and that this Esteem is only to be procured by beneficent Actions, and an inward Concern manifested by his outward Actions for the Good of others. (Johnson 1731: 40)[104]

---

[102] Appeals to the association of ideas in eighteenth-century British philosophy can often be traced back to Locke's account of association (*Essay* II.xxx) that he added to the fourth edition of his *Essay* in 1700. When Locke speaks of the association of ideas he is not merely concerned with connections among several simple ideas, but rather, as Tabb argues, those 'collections of simple ideas that are not connected in nature but which come to be connected in the mind in a way that brings with them a false judgment about reality' (2019: 92). Although bad habits can lead to the formation of associated ideas, bad habits – in contrast to associations of ideas that are mental pathologies for Locke – can be corrected (Tabb 2022). Following Locke, several eighteenth-century philosophers consider associations of ideas, but the exact meaning of association tends to shift and not all of them adopt Locke's view that association is a mental pathology. For further discussion, see Gill (1996), Warren (1921). Gay regards associations of ideas as habits. Thereby he shifts the meaning of association and has a more positive understanding of it than Locke. Cockburn is aware of this shift of meaning and comments on it in RSW 112.

[103] See Johnson (1731: 35–41).   [104] Quoted in Cockburn, RSW 123–4.

In Johnson's view such upbringing leads humans to desire the happiness of others and to associate pleasure with it. Once such an association is formed, 'whenever he contemplates the Happiness of another, he approves, or is pleas'd with it, without Reference to any farther End' (Johnson 1731: 40). According to Johnson, 'this Benevolence is rooted in our Minds' (1731: 40) and we tend to forget its actual origin and thus consider it as natural 'and act upon it as a Principle entirely distinct from Self-love' (1731: 41).

Cockburn is not convinced by Gay's and Johnson's arguments that all benevolent actions can ultimately be traced back to private happiness. For her their views are based on imaginary speculation that are out of touch with real world experience. According to Cockburn, 'there are many instances of benevolent affections; and a disinterested approbation of virtue, that cannot be accounted for by any supposed *association of ideas*' (RSW 113). For example, a mother's 'concern for the happiness of her child' (RSW 124), or acts of kindness among relatives, friends, or neighbours (Correspondence 237) are expressions of disinterested benevolence in Cockburn's view. Moreover, she rejects Gay's view that reason informs individuals to pursue their self-interest. Rather, according to Cockburn, the contrary is the case: 'right reason will inform him, that it is suitable to the nature of such a being, and worthy of approbation, to do all the good he can do for others, whether his own advantage is included in it or not' (RSW 114).

Additionally, she offers several considerations that challenge Johnson's assumption that benevolent affections are acquired through education. First of all, she points out that benevolent affections would be much rarer than they actually are if they presupposed education (RSW 124). On the contrary, she argues that those who have not been able to improve their understanding or who rarely make use of their reasoning capacities 'will perhaps be often found to have the strongest affections' (RSW 124). She vehemently rejects the view that benevolent affections presuppose education and claims:

> Men need not be *taught*, they *feel*, that their happiness is not independent of that of others; they find themselves unavoidably involved, or affected with the miseries of others, and can form no idea of happiness, into which some kind of communication with others does not enter. The very supposition of being happy alone, without regard to any person in the world, or whilst all about him were miserable, must appear a contradiction to a social nature: But this dependence of his happiness on that of others is the *effect* of his benevolent affections, not the *cause or ground* of them. (RSW 124)

Cockburn's *Remarks upon the Principles and Reasonings of Dr. Rutherforth* provide further insight into her thinking about self-interest, self-love, and benevolence. In this work she critically engages with Rutherforth's view that humans only pursue their own private happiness.[105] Although Rutherforth believes that all our actions arise from self-interest, for the sake of argument, he is willing to consider the possibility that moral goodness is a quality that makes us desire everyone's happiness (Rutherforth 1744: 64–65). If this was the case, Rutherforth argues, then as soon as we do good for others our own self-love would also increase. In his words, 'the more we practice moral good, the more we must desire our own happiness; we must grow selfish in proportion as we are virtuous; and be the more interested, the more benevolent we are' (Rutherforth 1744: 65).[106] Rutherforth argues further that this leads to a dilemma:

> Either . . . our sense of moral good and our affection for it do not reach to our own behaviour . . . or else the practice of virtue must be fatal to itself by strengthening that self-love which is represented by these very moralists as the only thing, that can stop the operation of the public affections, and keep the balance always inclined towards the side of private interest. (Rutherforth 1744: 65)[107]

Cockburn rejects Rutherforth's presupposition that one's selfishness increases proportional to the degree to which one does good for others. She claims that Rutherforth and some other moralists are mistaken to assume that self-love '*solely* regards private interest, exclusively of all public affections' (RR 158). Self-love for Cockburn does not have to exclude a 'concern for the good of any other' (RR 158). According to her, Rutherforth and some other writers have failed to consider 'self-love as a part of our nature, and consequently the work of God' (RR 158). As a consequence, they failed to see 'that true self-love and social are the same' (RR 158).

Cockburn specifies further that this error arises due to an 'ambiguity of words', namely a failure to realize 'that *self-love* is not *selfishness*' (RR 159). She argues that there is a kind of self-love which arises from our approval of our own behaviour and which can increase by doing morally good actions for others. This means that self-love can provide a natural inclination that motivates us to continue to interact benevolently with others. She rejects Rutherforth's claim that virtue will be fatal to itself and argues instead that by strengthening our self-love we in return also strengthen our virtue. She writes:

> Finding thus our happiness in that of others; virtue and self-love will go hand in hand together, and mutually support each other. We are, therefore, secure enough from growing *selfish* and *interested*, by the practice and approbation

---

[105] See especially Rutherforth (1744: chs. 7 and 8) and Cockburn, RR 159.
[106] Quoted in Cockburn, RR 158.   [107] Quoted in Cockburn, RR 158.

of a *disinterested benevolence*; and now may the better go on to enquire, whether there is really any such thing in nature. (RR 159)

While Cockburn rejects the view that benevolent actions, namely actions that promote the good of others, arise solely from self-interest or selfishness, she distinguishes self-love from selfishness and emphasizes that self-love and benevolence do not exclude each other.[108] Indeed, she believes that self-love can support and strengthen benevolence, as she states in the following passage:

> It is, I think, allowed by all, that every man's *first* care should be for his own good. *Charity begins at home*, is a maxim, not only of *fact*, but of *right*, implying, that it ought to do so. But then, if charity *ends* at home too, this indeed men are unwilling and ashamed to confess, and with very good reason, first, because it is not true, that men are generally unconcerned about every-body's happiness but their own; and next, because it is a very blameable selfishness, where this is the case. (RR 204)

4 Religion

Cockburn was deeply interested in religious questions and also a practising Christian. In previous sections we have seen how Cockburn assesses philosophical debates, for instance on topics in metaphysics or moral philosophy by comparing the plausibility of each position and evaluating the evidence for and against the different options. Her approach to religious questions is similar. For example, before she decided to convert back to Anglicanism, she carefully examined both the Catholic and the Protestant faiths and documented her reasons for preferring Protestantism in *A Discourse Concerning a Guide in Controversies* (*Works* 1:2–42). Cockburn questions claims of the Roman Catholic Church to be an infallible guide. Instead, she sides with the Protestant view 'that there is no infallible guide but Scripture' (*Works* 1:10).[109] Cockburn was a careful reader of the Bible and often turns to Scripture as her guide in religious questions. She further believes that religion should be rational and not conflict with reason, as becomes clear, for instance, in her criticism of mystic religious practices. Section 4.1 aims to shed further light on how she understands the relation between morality and religion and Section 4.2 turns to her beliefs in the resurrection and the afterlife.

4.1 Morality and Religion

In Section 3.1 we have seen that Cockburn argues that human nature is 'the first ground' of morality. This suggests that she believes that morality can be

---

[108] See Cockburn, RR 158–63, 204–5, *Works* 2:129–31, and Correspondence 236–8, 248–9.
[109] See also her 'On the Infallibility of the Church of Rome', in *Works* 2:134–8.

established independently of religious beliefs. Nevertheless, throughout her moral writings we find biblical references and this raises the question how and to what extent her religious beliefs shape her moral thinking. For instance, she regards the golden rule, namely the rule '*To do unto all men, as we would they should do unto me*', as 'the most perfect rule of life' and 'the sum of all the social virtues' (RR 152). In the following sections, we will consider whether and how Cockburn can, on the one hand, argue that morality can be established independently of religion but, on the other hand, also claim that religious practices, and particularly those rooted in Christianity, can be beneficial to morality.

4.1.1 Virtue of Atheists

Cockburn is one of very few philosophers of her day who defends the view that atheists can be virtuous (RSW 137–43).[110] She is concerned that if it is not possible for atheists to acquire moral knowledge, as Warburton (1738: 42) claims, then it would not be possible to blame or punish atheists for any misdeeds they may commit (RSW 137, 143). To further investigate the question of whether atheists can acquire moral knowledge independently of a belief in God's existence, Cockburn invites us to consider a society of atheists. She assumes that one of them is 'fallen into a pit, where he must inevitably perish if unassisted; and another of them happening to travel that way, who could with great ease relieve him' (RSW 138 n.). Cockburn is convinced that there is a '*natural* essential difference between leaving a man to perish in a pit, and helping him out of it' (RSW 138 n.), and she finds it hard to believe that the man who passes by would not be aware of this difference:

> Would not the distressed consider one of these as inhumanity to be detested, and the other as a good action deserving grateful return? Might not the traveler be too conscious, that one of these actions would be better than the other, have a goodness in it more to be approved? (RSW 138 n.)

Cockburn is convinced that humans irrespective of their religious beliefs are able to recognize moral differences such as in the case where one has a choice to save the life of a fellow human being or to let him die. Moreover, she believes that the advantage of her view is that atheists can be punished for their misdeeds, and she challenges her opponents to consider whether they are willing to admit

---

[110] Before Cockburn, Pierre Bayle had argued that a society of virtuous atheists is possible and is criticized for it by Warburton in *Divine Legation* (1738). Cockburn's defence of the virtue of atheists targets Warburton's position. The more widely held position that atheists cannot be virtuous was defended not just by Warburton, but also, for instance, by Locke in his *Letter concerning Toleration*. For helpful further discussion, see Broad (2021).

that, on their view, 'an Atheist is not accountable in a future state for any enormities he may commit here' (RSW 143).

4.1.2 Reason, Education, and Revelation

As Cockburn's discussion of the virtue of atheists illustrates, she is convinced that humans can acquire knowledge of morality by reflection on human nature. One advantage of her view is that anyone who is able to use reason and reflection can come to understand what is suitable or fitting for humans to do and this enables them to understand their moral obligations, irrespective of access to education or revelation.

Let us take a closer look at why Cockburn believes that education is not needed for becoming a moral agent. Cockburn argues against Rutherforth that we do not need a 'guide to teach us what our happiness, and what our duty is' (RR 207). She acknowledges that it can be useful and advantageous to have 'an infallible guide, to teach him plainly the way he should choose, and the end, to which it leads' (RR 207). However, she points out that not everyone is in a position to turn to a guide. Some people, perhaps due to unfortunate circumstances, may live in parts of the world where nobody is around who can teach them how to improve morally. In such circumstances, Cockburn argues, 'they can only consider what course of action their nature directs them to, as most likely to bring them safely to the end they were designed for' (RR 207). In her view nature and reason provide a sufficient guide and can teach us what our happiness and duty is (RR 207–8).

It is worth noting that Cockburn does not deny the usefulness of education. Indeed, in her essay 'On the Usefulness of Schools and Universities' (*Works* 2:125–7), she acknowledges that 'the establishment of schools and universities for the instruction of youth in the most useful sciences' (*Works* 2:125) is very advantageous and assumes that this is obvious to everyone 'who have had the happiness of a liberal education in them' (*Works* 2:215). She then adds a further consideration:

> I would only observe to you, that the greatest benefit we can receive from them, is by opening and enlarging our minds, to bring us to the knowledge of a supreme being, upon the most solid and rational grounds. This is the only immovable foundation of moral virtue; and without this all our other studies are vain and empty, I had almost said, pernicious speculations. (*Works* 2:125)

This remark highlights that knowledge of God plays a central role for her in education. In her view education should aim to open and enlarge the minds of young people and this is best done by 'bring[ing] us to the knowledge of a supreme being, upon the most solid and rational grounds' (*Works* 2:125).

She regards knowledge of God as central because she believes that all other sciences – including logic, astronomy, philosophy, and ethics – originate from or are related to God and would be 'vain and empty' if we lacked knowledge of God. For instance, to support her view that logic builds upon knowledge of God, she explains that logical reasoning processes 'cannot be the effect of senseless matter' (*Works* 2:125). She claims further that it follows from this that there must be 'an eternal, self-existent mind, from which all other thinking beings must be derived' (*Works* 2:125).

Let us consider her claim that knowledge of God 'is the only immovable foundation of moral virtue' (*Works* 2:125). One may worry that this claim conflicts with her view that atheists can be virtuous and, more generally, with her view that human nature is the first ground or foundation of morality. She adds the following considerations: 'And even in the practical sciences, he, who makes ethics his study, who considers the laws of nature, and the duties of society, if he leaves out of the consideration a supreme being, of perfect goodness and rectitude, will find he builds on a very defective foundation' (*Works* 2:126). Cockburn acknowledges that 'virtue is indeed lovely in itself, commands our approbation, and naturally tends to the happiness of mankind if universally practised' (*Works* 2:126). However, her concern is that if virtue is not considered in relation to God, humans can easily be disappointed and not attain the happiness that they expected for themselves or others. She worries that this could pose a risk for the stable practice of virtue, because someone who leaves out considerations of God 'has nothing left but the approbation of his own mind; and even that will begin to fail him, when he sees the aim and purpose of virtue defeated' (*Works* 2:126). In her view these problems are remedied if we turn to God:

> But if, from his ideas of goodness, justice, and equity, he has raised his thoughts to the original of those ideas, the author of that nature of ours, which is so formed, that we cannot but approve the practice of virtue, nor attain to our perfection or happiness without it; he will then have a noble and rational support against all difficulties and discouragements. (*Works* 2:126)

Upon closer consideration, it becomes clear that Cockburn's claims in her essay 'On the Usefulness of Schools and Universities' do not conflict with her view that atheists can be virtuous, since she is concerned about the stable *practice* of morality. In her view, knowledge of God and his will offers helpful further motivation and makes it more likely that we will stay on the path of virtue and attain happiness (*Works* 2:126–7).[111]

---

[111] Cockburn makes a similar point in 'Letter of Advice to Her Son', in *Works* 2:111.

Let us now turn to the further question, namely what, if any, role revelation plays in her philosophy. Cockburn rejects the view that revelation is required for moral knowledge. This helps her to distance herself from the views of theological voluntarists who believe that God can decide what is good and evil by an act of divine will.[112]

Moreover, she cautions against blind reliance on revelation, because this could open the door to enthusiasm (Broad 2020: 119–20; Correspondence 144–5, 153, 181). The term 'enthusiasm' is used in the early modern period to refer to misguided religious convictions and special inspirations, which can find expression in fanatic practices and superstition.[113] Cockburn, like many of her philosophical contemporaries, warns against the dangers of enthusiasm. Her correspondence with Arbuthnot sheds good light on Cockburn's reasons for rejecting enthusiasm. Cockburn and Arbuthnot discuss mystic writers in several of their letters, and Cockburn cautions Arbuthnot against mysticism, because she regards it as a form of enthusiasm. According to Jacqueline Broad, all the mystical authors that Arbuthnot and Cockburn discuss in their letters 'take a common mystical approach to religion; that is to say, they assent to the truth of religious claims on the basis of private ("mystical") experience of divine revelation' (2020: 119).

Cockburn claims that she 'could never find any solidity in [the mystics], and however the heart may be affected, if the understanding does not go along with it, tis to be feared the impressions will not be very lasting' (Correspondence 252). In a letter to Arbuthnot from 22 June 1738, Cockburn comments critically on Wolf von Metternich's book *Faith and Reason Compared*, which contains writings by several mystic authors (Broad 2020: 178 n. 253):

> the whole Doctrine of the Book opens a way to the wildest Enthusiasm, and leaves no defence against the delusions of seducing spirits, or a warm imagination, reason being utterly exploded, and declared incapable to judge of Divine things: for though I make no doubt that when God is pleased to reveal himself internally to the mind of man (as he has done on extraordinary occasions) he can do it in such a manner as to give a clear certainty that he is the Author of the Revelation; but this is no security against the delusions of other spirits, or of our own imaginations, if we unwarrantably give up our minds to expect Divine illuminations, and are perswaded that Reason must not presume to examine whether they are Divine or not. One would think these Mystick writers scarce look upon Reason as a gift of the All-wise God,

---

[112] See Section 3.3 above for further discussion of Cockburn's arguments against theological voluntarism.

[113] For instance, Locke criticizes enthusiasm in *Essay* IV.xix. See Boespflug and Pasnau (2022) for further discussion. Shaftesbury (2001 [1711]: 1:1–36) is another critic of enthusiasm.

but rather of some Evil Principle, so much they fear to be guided by it. (Correspondence 181)

Cockburn worries that it is dangerous to disconnect reason from religion. In her view, reason has a role to play in religious beliefs and has to examine their credibility; otherwise, delusions and imaginary beliefs could be presented in the name of religion. She expresses similar concerns in another letter to Arbuthnot (then Hepburn), dated 2 March 1733 (Correspondence 144–6). In this letter she emphasizes that morality and religion should not be treated as distinct from each other. In Cockburn's view, to regard moral virtue as distinct from religion is 'the most pernicious error in the world, and ... has given rise to the greatest superstitions and the wildest fanaticism that the head of man is capable of' (Correspondence 144). Enthusiasts who claimed that God's will is separate from morality 'committed the most extravagant outrages, and the blackest villanies, under the pretence of serving the cause of God' (Correspondence 144). To prevent massacres in the name of religion and other misuses of religion, Cockburn advocates for a rational religion that leaves scope for reason to check religious beliefs for contradictions and inconsistencies. Moreover, she believes that religion and morality should not be separated.

It is worth noting that Cockburn does not claim that all religious beliefs can be discovered by reason, but rather she accepts that some beliefs are a matter of revelation and cannot be explained by other means. She comments on this issue as follows in her 'Notes on Christianity as Old as the Creation':

> Though it be true, that nothing could be admitted for divine revelation, that contradicted our natural notions of good and evil, or inconsistent with the demonstrable attributes of God; yet it does not follow, that nothing can be matter of revelation, but what reason could antecedently discover. There are many truths, which may be very useful forms to know, which reason could by no means assure us of, though very consistent with it when revealed; for instance, God's acceptance of penitent sinners, and the resurrection of the dead. (*Works* 2:133)

4.1.3 Christianity and Morality

Cockburn was a Christian believer. As we have already seen, she accepts that in principle atheists can be virtuous, but as far as the practice of morality is concerned, she believes it is advantageous to believe in God. Since God's will coincides with the moral fitnesses that arise from the natures of things, God's will can offer additional motivation to act morally. It remains to consider whether any religion can support morality or whether for Cockburn the Christian faith plays a special role in strengthening morality.

In a manuscript note, titled 'Sunday's Journal', Cockburn emphasizes how important it is that a religious life manifests itself in moral actions in this world:

> Among the many mistakes and false notions concerning religion, I know none, that more generally prevails, than that of considering it as a thing so entirely distinct from the common actions and affairs of life, as to have nothing at all to do with them, and placing the whole of religion in one single branch of it. From this partial view and mistaken notion, numbers, who have been convinced of the necessity of leading a religious life, have thought it necessary to seclude themselves from the world. (*Works* 2:121–2)

Cockburn is not shy to criticize secluded religious life, for instance in monasteries, that focuses on contemplation and prayer but fails to take seriously that Jesus 'their great master, (who surely best understood his own religion) both practised, and taught, and strongly enforced justice, charity, meekness, forgiveness, and all the social virtues' (*Works* 2:122).

Cockburn's correspondence with Arbuthnot provides further insight into how proper Christian faith can strengthen morality. In several of their letters, they discuss Shaftesbury's philosophy, but Cockburn takes a more critical stance towards Shaftesbury's philosophy than Arbuthnot.[114] It is worth considering why Cockburn distances her views from Shaftesbury's philosophy. Although Shaftesbury accepts that religion can provide useful support to morality, he was a harsh critic of Christian beliefs, and especially beliefs in divine reward and punishment (Shaftesbury 2001 [1711]). Cockburn does not share Shaftesbury's criticism of the Christian religion and claims that Shaftesbury, like several other moralists, was prejudiced 'against the Doctrines of the Gospel' (Correspondence 205). Cockburn, by contrast, believes that 'the purest morality is to be found' (Correspondence 205) in the Gospel. Cockburn comments further on Shaftesbury's prejudices against Christianity in another letter to Arbuthnot from 12 June 1744:

> I dont know from whence his prejudices arose, but if it was from the violencies, divisions, or degeneracy of Christians, surely a man of his penetration might have known mankind well enough to conclude that the best Religion in such hands must be mingled with the passions, frailties and mistakes of men, and should not have thought it reasonable to condemn the Purest Principles, for the sake of practices entirely opposite to them: could he know the world, and think that morality, and by consequence the good of his country, would be less advanced by the Belief of Christianity (even with his hard thoughts of its Teachers) than by no Religion at all? Without which it has

---

[114] Cockburn and Arbuthnot discuss Shaftesbury's philosophy in several of their letters, including in Correspondence 142, 144, 178–9, 182, 183, 201, 205, 208–9, 213–14, 216, 223, 225, 229–30, 231–2, 235–6, 245, 249–51.

never been thought practicable in any age, or country, to keep up any tolerable order in society. If instead of that he proposed to bring the Bulk of Mankind to a love of virtue for its Beauty, and excellencies, and to give them all his own refined Taste; he might as well (as a great author says) have proposed to make them all Lords. (Correspondence 213–14)

Cockburn criticizes Shaftesbury for renouncing Christian beliefs and is convinced that the Christian religion is more suitable to ensure the practice of morality than Shaftesbury's aristocratic views that morality and beauty are one and the same and form a harmonious whole (Shaftesbury 2001 [1711]: 2:223).[115] Cockburn is more drawn to Joseph Butler's moral philosophy in his *Sermons* (2017) and recommends that Arbuthnot reads Butler's *Sermons* to better understand the shortcomings of Shaftesbury's philosophy (Correspondence 182).

As already noted, Cockburn regards the Gospel as a particularly important biblical source for the practice of morality. We find further evidence for this in her 'Notes on Christianity as Old as Creation', where she states that 'the whole tenor of the Gospel is a declaration of the exceeding love of God to mankind, and the strongest motive of love and gratitude to him; nor is there any thing superadded to natural religion in all the doctrines of it, but greater incitements or assistances to the performance of moral duties' (*Works* 2:134). As she states here, the Gospel offers helpful assistance and a stronger motivation to perform our moral duties.

4.2 Resurrection and the Afterlife

As a Christian, Cockburn believes that there will be a resurrection of the dead, but she also acknowledges that this cannot be demonstrated by reason and is a matter of divine revelation (*Works* 2:133). Cockburn had already engaged with questions concerning immortality and the afterlife in her first philosophical work *Defence*,[116] but she gives the topic, and especially questions concerning the resurrection of the dead, more detailed consideration in her *Letter to Dr. Holdsworth* (1727) and her subsequent *Vindication of Mr. Locke's Christian Principles* (1751).

Cockburn and Holdsworth disagree whether the Bible supports that there will be a resurrection of the same body, as Holdsworth claims, or merely a resurrection of the dead, as Cockburn, following Locke, argues. Much of their dispute rests on exegetical questions of how to interpret the Bible.[117] Locke and Cockburn adopt the stance that something that is not revealed in

---

[115] See Gill (2022) for further discussion.   [116] See Section 2.2.
[117] For helpful further discussion of these exegetical issues, see Chatterjee (2020).

Scripture cannot be a matter of faith. Holdsworth challenges Locke's minimalist reading of the Bible and argues that biblical texts should be considered in their historical context and that interpreters must have sufficient knowledge of the original languages. In this vein, Holdsworth writes:

> A *False* Method of *Interpreting Scripture* is *another* great *Fault* of *Men* and *Times*, by which, *This*, and *other* Articles of *Faith* have been *Corrupted*, *Disputed*, and *Deny'd*. For it is not by any means to be Allow'd, that where any Man Hath a competent Knowledge of the *Original* Languages, and *sufficient* Abilities of Understanding to *Interpret* or *Explain* the Scriptures, that He is then *perfectly* Qualify'd to *Undertake* it. (Holdsworth 1720: 23)

Although Holdsworth acknowledges that the Bible explicitly only speaks of the resurrection of the dead, he turns to old church texts to show that the authors of these texts interpret the resurrection to be a resurrection of the same body. Thus, Holdsworth believes that once the biblical texts are properly understood in their historical context we have good evidence to assume that there will be a resurrection of the same body in the vulgar sense of sameness. Holdsworth distinguishes the vulgar sense of sameness from 'mathematical' sameness, or strict numerical identity, and accepts that the resurrected body does not have to be composed of all of the same particles that composed the human body during this life (Holdsworth 1720: 7–9).

Cockburn mentions that Locke has addressed many of the issues raised by Holdsworth in his correspondence with Edward Stillingfleet (Locke 1823: vol. 4). She makes clear that the question for Locke is whether the resurrection of the same body is revealed in Scripture (*Letter to Holdsworth* 127–8). Since Scripture only speaks of the resurrection of the dead and remains silent on whether they will be resurrected with the same body or not, Locke is cautious not to make any claims that are unsupported by Scripture (*Letter to Holdsworth* 133–6).

Although Cockburn's main aim in her *Letter to Holdsworth* and her *Vindication* is to defend Locke against Holdsworth's charges, I want to highlight how her account of the resurrection is not merely a restatement of Locke's position, but rather sheds light on her own thinking about the resurrection and the relation between mind and body. Locke might have responded to Holdsworth that persons rather than men or substances will be resurrected and it is not relevant to know whether persons will be resurrected with the same body. Although Cockburn acknowledges Locke's distinctions between the ideas of person, man, and soul or substance, she does not defend Locke by arguing for the resurrection of persons. Instead she argues that the dispute between Locke and Holdsworth is to a significant extent a verbal dispute and draws attention to how similar their views are upon closer inspection (*Letter to Holdsworth* 132).[118]

First of all, Cockburn points out that Locke in his correspondence with Stillingfleet, which builds on his discussion of personal identity in *Essay* II. xxvii, uses the term 'body' in a different sense than Holdsworth uses it. Locke understands sameness of body in terms of numerical identity of particles and believes that as soon as particles are added to or subtracted from a body this body ceases to be the body it was before the change of particles. Holdsworth, by contrast, uses 'body' in a looser sense and allows that a body can continue to exist over time despite changes of particles and claims that a '*Humane* Body is therefore unexceptionably the *same*, as long as it *continues* Distinct, *from all other* Bodies of it's *own*, or a *different* Species: whatever *Successions* of Matter in it's Course of Life, 'till Death, it may run through' (Holdsworth 1720: 7–8). Since Locke challenges Stillingfleet's assumption that the resurrected being must be composed of numerically identical particles as a human being before death by pointing out that the particles that compose the human body constantly change, Cockburn believes that Locke 'had just the same thoughts about the resurrection-body' (*Letter to Holdsworth* 133) as Holdsworth. She claims further that they 'both assert that it may consist of part of the old materials, with some new particles added to them' (*Letter to Holdsworth* 133).

Cockburn goes a step further and argues that a belief in the resurrection entails more than merely the belief 'that an unembodied spirit, such as is the soul when separated from the body, continues to live elsewhere' (*Letter to Holdsworth* 150). Indeed, she even claims that 'that can, by no construction of words, be called a resurrection of the dead' (*Letter to Holdsworth* 150). Instead, her view is that 'the raising must be understood of that which died, the same species, a creature consisting of soul and body: the same man must be raised at the last day; otherwise there is no resurrection of the dead' (*Letter to Holdsworth* 150). She suggests that this shows how close Locke's view comes to Holdsworth's. However, I want to suggest that this passage can be better seen as evidence of Cockburn's own independent thinking about the resurrection. She claims that the resurrected individual must be a member of the same species as the individual that was alive on earth. This is a plausible assumption to make but leads to the question, which species is the best candidate for being resurrected? Will human beings (or men) be resurrected? Will persons be resurrected? Will souls be resurrected? Or will members of some other species be resurrected? Cockburn is quick to claim that 'the same man must be raised at the

---

[118] Holdsworth (1727: 153–61) denies that their dispute is verbal.

last day' (*Letter to Holdsworth* 150). Locke may dispute this and argue that it is more likely that the same person rather than the same man will be resurrected.

The fact that Cockburn does not consider these other options could be a sign that she is immersed in her own philosophical thinking. As we have seen in previous sections, human nature plays a fundamental role in her moral philosophy and reflection on human nature provides moral and religious knowledge. When Cockburn reflects on human nature, she examines the nature of beings that are sensible, rational, and social, and thus have minds and bodies. Perhaps her moral theory is in the background of her religious beliefs and helps explain her religious belief that a man or human being 'consisting of soul and body' (*Letter to Holdsworth* 150) will be resurrected.

5 Cockburn's Significance

Cockburn cleverly and intelligently engaged with the philosophical debates of her day and made important contributions of her own to questions concerning epistemology, metaphysics, moral philosophy, and philosophy of religion. Her philosophical enquiries are guided by sensation and reflection, which she regards as the sources of knowledge, and she takes seriously the limitations of human understanding. Cockburn carefully examines and assesses the evidence for and against the different philosophical views defended by her contemporaries, and she is not shy to challenge views that were widely held by other philosophers of her day.[119]

Cockburn's philosophical writings received the praise of several of her philosophical contemporaries.[120] For instance, Elizabeth Berkeley Burnet, in her correspondence with Locke, draws his attention to Cockburn's anonymously published *Defence* and reveals the author's name and address to him. Locke expresses his gratitude in a letter to Cockburn, dated 30 December 1702, and acknowledges 'the strength and clearness of [her] reasoning' (Locke 1976–89: 7:731). Locke writes further, 'You have herein not only vanquished my adversary, but reduced me also absolutely under your power, and left no desires more strong in me, than those of meeting with some opportunity' (Locke 1976–89: 7:731). James Tyrrell also thinks highly about Cockburn's *Defence* and writes to Locke on 25 July 1703: 'I have read the Gentlewomans Defence of your Essay, etc against the cavilling Animadverter and am so well pleas'd with it, that I think none but your self could have performed it better' (Locke 1976–89: letter 3324, 8:44). Moreover, Leibniz mentions Cockburn's *Defence* in his

---

[119] For instance, she questions that souls perpetually think and argues in support of the thinking matter hypothesis (see Section 2.2).

[120] For further discussion, see Bolton (1993), Kelley (2002).

New Essays, which is Leibniz's section by section response to Locke's *Essay*.
New Essays is a dialogue between Philalethes, who presents Locke's views, and
Theophilus, who presents Leibniz's views. Through the voice of Philalethes,
Leibniz states that 'I enjoyed reading a defence of him [i.e. Locke] by
a judicious and insightful young lady' (Leibniz 1996: I.i.70). The Irish philosopher John Toland also took note of *Defence* and in the preface to his *Letters to
Serena* he describes the author as 'a lady not personally known to me, who is
absolute mistress of the most abstracted speculations in the metaphysics, and
who with an early turn of style and argument has defended Mr Locke's *Essay of
human understanding*, against the letters of an eminent divine' (Toland 2013
[1704]: Preface, 52).

Cockburn's works were also read and discussed by members of the
Bluestocking circle and inspired their writings. The Bluestocking circle developed from the activities of a group of female friends who had shared interests in
literature and other intellectual matters and flourished in England during
the second half of the eighteenth century. Its members encouraged and sup-
ported each other's writings and intellectual endeavours.[121] Elizabeth Carter
and Catherine Talbot, the oldest members of the Bluestocking circle, discuss
Cockburn's writings in their correspondence.[122] For instance, Talbot writes to
Carter on 27 September 1751: 'I love Mrs. Cockburn dearly for her zeal in
defending him [i.e. Pope]. She seems to have had an honest, upright, affection-
ate heart, that I honour. What a pity that her last years were in a manner lost in
obscurity so little suited to her genius' (Carter 1809: 2:52). Talbot here not only
acknowledges Cockburn's intellectual 'genius' and her admirable personal
character, but she is also concerned about the challenges that she faced as
a female writer. Having witnessed how Cockburn has not received as much
recognition as she deserved during her lifetime, Talbot is concerned that other
women writers such as Elizabeth Carter may suffer a similar fate.[123]

Elizabeth Montagu, another member of the Bluestocking circle developed
a friendship with Cockburn's niece Ann Arbuthnot and speaks highly of both
Arbuthnot and Cockburn in her correspondence with James Beattie. In a letter to
Beattie from 17 September 1784, Montagu goes so far as to call Cockburn the
'great Diamond of her Sex'.[124]

Cockburn had extensive familiarity with the debates in British moral philosophy during the first half of the eighteenth century. In her philosophical

---

[121] For further discussion of the Bluestockings and their engagement with Cockburn, see Green
(2014), Myers (1990), Sheridan (2018b).

[122] See Carter (1809: 2:49–50, 52).   [123] For further details, see Bigold (2013: 142).

[124] Elizabeth Montagu Correspondence Online, Swansea University, https://emco.swansea.ac.uk/
emco/letter-view/1849/, accessed 30 September 2022.

writings she discusses not only the moral theories of relatively well known British moralists such as Shaftesbury, Hutcheson, Butler, and Clarke, but also authors whose writings have received less attention in twentieth and twenty-first century histories of British moral philosophy such as Law, Gay, Johnson, Warburton, and Rutherforth. Interestingly, all authors of this latter group had affiliations with the University of Cambridge at certain stages of their lives and their network and contributions to British moral philosophy has not yet been sufficiently studied. To the present day, histories of British moral philosophy rarely acknowledge contributions by women philosophers such as Cockburn.[125] Her moral philosophy invites us to rethink the narratives of British moral philosophy and can also help us recover the writings and networks of other neglected philosophers and intellectuals.

---

[125] For instance, Crisp (2019), Darwall (1995), Gill (2006), Heydt (2018), Schneewind (1998), Stuart-Buttle (2019) portray the history of British moral philosophy as predominantly, if not exclusively, male. Irwin (2007: 2:835–8) briefly considers Cockburn's moral writings.

Abbreviations

References to seventeenth- and eighteenth-century works follow common referencing conventions and are abbreviated and cited in the following formats.

Works by Catharine Trotter Cockburn

Correspondence
(2020) 'Catharine Trotter Cockburn (1679?–1749)'. In *Women Philosophers of Eighteenth-Century England: Selected Correspondence*, edited by J. Broad, 116–265. New York: Oxford University Press.

Defence
(2006 [1702]) *A Defence of Mr. Locke's Essay of Human Understanding*. Edited by P. Sheridan. Peterborough, ON: Broadview Press.

Letter to Holdsworth
(1751 [1727]) *A Letter to Dr. Holdsworth*. In vol. 1 of *The Works of Mrs. Catharine Cockburn*, edited by T. Birch, 113–53. London: Printed for J. and P. Knapton.

RR
(2006 [1747]) *Remarks upon the Principles and Reasonings of Dr. Rutherforth's Essay on the Nature and Obligation of Virtue*. Edited by P. Sheridan. Peterborough, ON: Broadview Press.

RSW
(2006 [1743]) *Remarks upon Some Writers in the Controversy Concerning the Foundation of Moral Virtue and Moral Obligation*. Edited by P. Sheridan. Peterborough, ON: Broadview Press.

Vindication
(1751) *A Vindication of Mr. Locke's Christian Principles*. In vol. 1 of *The Works of Mrs. Catharine Cockburn*, edited by T. Birch, 155–378. London: Printed for J. and P. Knapton.

Works
(1751) *The Works of Mrs. Catharine Cockburn*. Edited by T. Birch. 2 vols. London: Printed for J. and P. Knapton.

Works by René Descartes

AT
(1964–76) *Ouvres de Descartes*. Edited by C. Adam and P. Tannery. 12 vols. Paris: J. Vrin.

CSM (1984–5) *The Philosophical Writings of Descartes*. Translated and edited by J. Cottingham, R. Stoothoff, and D. Murdoch. Vols. 1 and 2 (out of 3 vols.). Cambridge: Cambridge University Press.

Works by John Locke

Essay (1975 [1690]) *An Essay Concerning Human Understanding*. Edited by P. H. Nidditch. Oxford: Clarendon Press. Cited by book, chapter, section number.

Anonymously Published Works

Remarks (1697a) *Remarks upon an Essay Concerning Humane Understanding in a Letter Address'd to the Author.* London: Printed for M. Wotton.

Second Remarks (1697b) *Second Remarks upon an Essay Concerning Humane Understanding in a Letter Address'd to the Author, Being a Vindication of the First Remarks against the Answer of Mr. Lock, at the End of His Reply to the Lord Bishop of Worcester.* London: Printed for M. Wotton.

Third Remarks (1699) *Third Remarks upon an Essay Concerning Humane Understanding in a Letter Address'd to the Author.* London: Printed for M. Wotton.

References

Anon. (1697a) *Remarks upon an Essay Concerning Humane Understanding in a Letter Address'd to the Author*. London: Printed for M. Wotton.

Anon. (1697b) *Second Remarks upon an Essay Concerning Humane Understanding in a Letter Address'd to the Author, Being a Vindication of the First Remarks against the Answer of Mr. Lock, at the End of His Reply to the Lord Bishop of Worcester*. London: Printed for M. Wotton.

Anon. (1699) *Third Remarks upon an Essay Concerning Humane Understanding in a Letter Address'd to the Author*. London: Printed for M. Wotton.

Anstey, P. R. (2013) '*Locke's Moral Man*, by Antonia LoLordo'. *Mind* 122 (488):1146–9.

Atherton, M. (2013) 'Antonia LoLordo, *Locke's Moral Man*'. *Notre Dame Philosophical Review*. https://ndpr.nd.edu/reviews/locke-s-moral-man/.

Bigold, M. (2013) *Women of Letters, Manuscript Circulation, and Print Afterlives in the Eighteenth Century: Elizabeth Rowe, Catharine Cockburn, and Elizabeth Carter*. Basingstoke, UK: Palgrave Macmillan.

Birch, T. (1751) 'The Life of Mrs. Catharine Cockburn'. In *The Works of Mrs. Catharine Cockburn*, edited by T. Birch, 1:i–xlviii. London: Printed for J. and P. Knapton.

Boeker, R. (2021a) 'Locke on Being Self to My Self'. In *The Self: A History*, edited by P. Kitcher, 118–44. New York: Oxford University Press.

Boeker, R. (2021b) *Locke on Persons and Personal Identity*. Oxford: Oxford University Press.

Boeker, R. (2022) 'Hutcheson and His Critics and Opponents on the Moral Sense'. *Journal of Scottish Philosophy* 20 (2):143–61.

Boespflug, M., and R. Pasnau (2022) 'Locke on Enthusiasm'. In *The Lockean Mind*, edited by J. Gordon-Roth and S. Weinberg, 554–63. Abingdon, UK: Routledge.

Bolton, M. B. (1993) 'Some Aspects of the Philosophical Work of Catharine Trotter'. *Journal of the History of Philosophy* 31 (4):565–88.

Bolton, M. B. (2016) 'Locke on Thinking Matter'. In *A Companion to Locke*, edited by M. Stuart, 334–53. Malden, MA: Wiley Blackwell.

Briscoe, S., ed. (1693) *Letters of Love and Gallantry and Several Other Subjects. All written by Ladies*. Vol. 1. London: Printed for S. Briscoe.

Broad, J. (2002) *Women Philosophers of the Seventeenth Century*. Cambridge: Cambridge University Press.

Broad, J. (2014) 'Women on Liberty in Early Modern England'. *Philosophy Compass* 9 (2):112–22.

Broad, J., ed. (2019) *Women Philosophers of Seventeenth-Century England: Selected Correspondence*. New York: Oxford University Press.

Broad, J., ed. (2020) *Women Philosophers of Eighteenth-Century England: Selected Correspondence*. New York: Oxford University Press.

Broad, J. (2021) 'Catharine Trotter Cockburn on the Virtue of Atheists'. *Intellectual History Review* 31 (1):111–28.

Butler, J. (2017) *Fifteen Sermons and Other Writings on Ethics*. Edited by D. McNaughton. Oxford: Oxford University Press.

Carter, E. (1809) *A Series of Letters between Mrs. Elizabeth Carter and Miss Catherine Talbot, from the Year 1741 to 1770, to Which Are Added, Letters from Mrs. Elizabeth Carter to Mrs. Vesey, between the Years 1763 and 1787*. 4 vols. London: Printed for F. C. and J. Rivington.

Chatterjee, J. D. (2020) 'Christian Antiquity and the Anglican Reception of John Locke's Paraphrase and Notes on the Epistles of St. Paul, 1707–1730'. *Locke Studies* 20:1–36.

Clarke, S. (1711 [1706]) *A Discourse Concerning the Unchangeable Obligations of Natural Religion, and the Truth and Certainty of the Christian Revelation*. 3rd ed. London: Printed by W. Botham, for J. Knapton.

Clarke, S. (1998 [1705]) *A Demonstration of the Being and Attributes of God and Other Writings*. Edited by E. Vailati. Cambridge: Cambridge University Press.

Cockburn, C. T. (1751) *The Works of Mrs. Catharine Cockburn*. Edited by T. Birch. 2 vols. London: Printed for J. and P. Knapton.

Cockburn, C. T. (1751 [1727]) *A Letter to Dr. Holdsworth*. In vol. 1 of *The Works of Mrs. Catharine Cockburn*, edited by T. Birch, 113–53. London: Printed for J. and P. Knapton.

Cockburn, C. T. (2006 [1702]) *A Defence of Mr. Locke's Essay of Human Understanding*. Edited by P. Sheridan. Peterborough, ON: Broadview Press.

Cockburn, C. T. (2006 [1743]) *Remarks upon Some Writers in the Controversy Concerning the Foundation of Moral Virtue and Moral Obligation*. Edited by P. Sheridan. Peterborough, ON: Broadview Press.

Cockburn, C. T. (2006 [1747]) *Remarks upon the Principles and Reasonings of Dr. Rutherforth's Essay on the Nature and Obligation of Virtue*. Edited by P. Sheridan. Peterborough, ON: Broadview Press.

Crisp, R. (2019) *Sacrifice Regained: Morality and Self-Interest in British Moral Philosophy from Hobbes to Bentham*. Oxford: Oxford University Press.

Darwall, S. (1995) *The British Moralists and the Internal 'Ought': 1640–1740.* Cambridge: Cambridge University Press.

De Tommaso, E. M. (2017) '"Some Reflections upon the True Grounds of Morality": Catharine Trotter in Defence of John Locke'. *Philosophy Study* 7 (6):326–39.

De Tommaso, E. M., and G. Mocchi. (2021) 'John Locke and Catharine Cockburn on Personal Identity'. *Rivista di storia della filosofia* (2021/2): 205–20.

Descartes, R. (1964–76) Ouvres de Descartes. Edited by C. Adam and P. Tannery. 12 vols. Paris: J. Vrin.

Descartes, R. (1984–91) *The Philosophical Writings of Descartes*. Translated and edited by J. Cottingham, R. Stoothoff, D. Murdoch, and A. Kenny. 3 vols. Cambridge: Cambridge University Press.

Duncan, S. (2022) *Materialism from Hobbes to Locke*. New York: Oxford University Press.

Gay, J. (1732 [1731]) 'Preliminary Dissertation Concerning the Fundamental Principle of Virtue or Morality'. In *An Essay on the Origin of Evil, by Dr. William King, Late Lord Archbishop of Dublin, Translated from the Latin, with Notes; and a Dissertation Concerning the Principle and Criterion of Virtue and the Origin of the Passions*, edited by E. Law, xxviii–lvii. London: Printed for W. Thurlbourn.

Gill, M. B. (1996) 'Fantastick Associations and Addictive General Rules: A Fundamental Difference between Hutcheson and Hume'. *Hume Studies* 22 (1):23–48.

Gill, M. B. (2006) *The British Moralists on Human Nature and the Birth of Secular Ethics*. Cambridge: Cambridge University Press.

Gill, M. B. (2022) *A Philosophy of Beauty: Shaftesbury on Nature, Virtue, and Art*. Princeton: Princeton University Press.

Gordon-Roth, J. (2015a) 'Catharine Trotter Cockburn's Defence of Locke'. *The Monist* 98 (1):64–76.

Gordon-Roth, J. (2015b) 'Locke on the Ontology of Persons'. *Southern Journal of Philosophy* 53 (1):97–123.

Green, K. (2014) *A History of Women's Political Thought in Europe, 1700–1800*. Cambridge: Cambridge University Press.

Green, K. (2015) 'A Moral Philosophy of Their Own? The Moral and Political Thought of Eighteenth-Century British Women'. *The Monist* 98 (1):89–101.

Green, K. (2019) 'On Some Footnotes to Catharine Trotter Cockburn's Defence of the Essay of Human Understanding'. *British Journal for the History of Philosophy* 27 (4):824–41.

Heydt, C. (2018) *Moral Philosophy in Eighteenth-Century Britain: God, Self, and Other*. Cambridge: Cambridge University Press.

Hobbes, T. (1994 [1651]) *Leviathan: With Selected Variants from the Latin Edition of 1668*. Edited by E. Curley. Indianapolis: Hackett.

Holdsworth, W. (1720) *A Sermon Preached before the University of Oxford at St Mary's on Easter-Monday, 1719*. London: Printed at the Theatre, for Rich. Wilkin at the King's Head in St Paul's Church Yard.

Holdsworth, W. (1727) *A Defence of the Doctrine of the Resurrection of the Same Body: In Two Parts*. London: Printed for C. Rivington.

Hutcheson, F. (2002 [1728]) *An Essay on the Nature and Conduct of the Passions and Affections, with Illustrations on the Moral Sense*. Edited by A. Garrett. Indianapolis: Liberty Fund.

Hutcheson, F. (2004 [1725]) *An Inquiry into the Original of Our Ideas of Beauty and Virtue*. Edited by W. Leidhold. Indianapolis: Liberty Fund.

Hutton, S. (2017) 'Liberty of the Mind: Women Philosophers and the Freedom to Philosophize'. In *Women and Liberty, 1600–1800: Philosophical Essays*, edited by J. Broad and K. Detlefsen, 123–37. Oxford: Oxford University Press.

Irwin, T. (2007) *The Development of Ethics: A Historical and Critical Study*. 3 vols. Oxford: Oxford University Press.

Johnson, T. (1731) *An Essay on Moral Obligation: With a View Towards Settling the Controversy, Concerning Moral and Positive Duties*. London: Printed by J. S. for W. Thurlbourn.

Johnston, G. (1732) *The Eternal Obligation of Natural Religion, or, The Foundation of Morality to God and Man: Being An Answer to Dr. Wright's Remarks upon Mr. Mole's Sermon*. London: Printed for T. Cox.

Jolley, N. (2015) *Locke's Touchy Subjects: Materialism and Immortality*. Oxford: Oxford University Press.

Kelley, A. (2002) *Catharine Trotter: An Early Modern Vanguard of Feminism*. Aldershot: Ashgate.

Kelley, A. (2004) 'Trotter [*married name* Cockburn], Catharine'. In *Oxford Dictionary of National Biography*. Oxford: Oxford University Press.

Kelley, A., ed. (2006a) *Catharine Trotter's The Adventures of a Young Lady and Other Works*. Adlershot: Ashgate.

Kelley, A. (2006b) 'Introductory Note'. In *Catharine Trotter's The Adventures of a Young Lady and Other Works*, edited by A. Kelley, vii–xiii. Adlershot: Ashgate.

Kim, H.-K. (2019) *Locke's Ideas of Mind and Body*. New York: Routledge.

Lascano, M. P. (2019) 'Women Philosophers and the Cosmological Argument: A Case Study in Feminist History of Philosophy'. In *Feminist History of Philosophy: The Recovery and Evaluation of Women's Philosophical Thought*, edited by E. O'Neill and M. P. Lascano, 23–47. Cham, Switz.: Springer.

Law, E., ed. (1732 [1731]) *An Essay on the Origin of Evil, by Dr. William King, Late Lord Archbishop of Dublin, Translated from the Latin, with Notes; and A Dissertation Concerning the Principle and Criterion of Virtue and the Origin of the Passions.* 2nd ed. London: Printed for W. Thurlbourn.

Law, E. (1769) *A Defence of Mr. Locke's Opinion Concerning Personal Identity; in Answer to the First Part of a Late Essay on That Subject.* Cambridge: Printed by J. Archdeacon.

Leibniz, G. W. (1996) *New Essays on Human Understanding.* Edited by P. Remnant and J. Bennett. Cambridge: Cambridge University Press.

Leisinger, M. A. (2019) 'Locke on Persons and Other Kinds of Substances'. *Pacific Philosophical Quarterly* 100 (1):129–55.

Locke, J. (1823) *The Works of John Locke.* New, corrected ed. 10 vols. London: Thomas Tegg.

Locke, J. (1976–89) *The Correspondence of John Locke.* Edited by E. S. de Beer. 8 vols. Oxford: Clarendon Press.

LoLordo, A. (2011) 'Person, Substance, Mode and "The Moral Man" in Locke's Philosophy'. *Canadian Journal of Philosophy* 40 (4):643–67.

LoLordo, A. (2012) *Locke's Moral Man.* Oxford: Oxford University Press.

LoLordo, A. (2013) 'Three Problems in Locke's Ontology of Substance and Mode'. In *Contemporary Perspectives on Early Modern Philosophy: Nature and Norms in Thought,* edited by M. Lenz and A. Waldow, 51–64. Dordrecht: Springer.

Lovejoy, A. O. (1936) *The Great Chain of Being.* Cambridge, MA: Harvard University Press.

Lucci, D. (2021) *Locke's Christianity.* Cambridge: Cambridge University Press.

Lustila, G. L. (2020) 'Catharine Trotter Cockburn's Democratization of Moral Virtue'. *Canadian Journal of Philosophy* 50 (1):83–97.

Mandeville, B. (1723 [1714]) *Fable of the Bees, or, Private Vices, Publick Benefits.* 2nd ed. London: Printed for E. Parker.

Maurer, C. (2019) *Self-love, Egoism and the Selfish Hypothesis: Key Debates from Eighteenth-Century British Moral Philosophy.* Edinburgh: Edinburgh University Press.

Millar, A. (1988) 'Following Nature'. *Philosophical Quarterly* 38 (151):165–85.

Miller, A. (2003) *An Introduction to Contemporary Metaethics.* Cambridge: Polity Press.

Montagu, E. (n.d.) Elizabeth Montagu Correspondence Online. Swansea University. https://emco.swansea.ac.uk.

Myers, J. E. (2012) 'Catharine Trotter and the Claims of Conscience'. *Tulsa Studies in Women's Literature* 31 (1–2):53–75.

Myers, S. H. (1990) *The Bluestocking Circle: Women, Friendship, and the Life of the Mind in Eighteenth-Century England*. Oxford: Clarendon Press.

Nuovo, V. (2011) *Christianity, Antiquity, and Enlightenment: Interpretations of Locke*. Dordrecht: Springer.

Ready, K. J. (2002) 'Damaris Cudworth Masham, Catharine Trotter Cockburn, and the Feminist Legacy of Locke's Theory of Personal Identity'. *Eighteenth-Century Studies* 35 (4):563–76.

Rickless, S. C. (2015) 'Are Locke's Persons Modes or Substances?' In *Locke and Leibniz on Substance*, edited by P. Lodge and T. Stoneham, 110–27. New York: Routledge.

Rickless, S. C. (2017) 'Locke's Ontology of Relations'. *Locke Studies* 17:61–86.

Rutherforth, T. (1744) *An Essay on the Nature and Obligations of Virtue*. Cambridge: Printed by J. Bentham.

Schneewind, J. B. (1998) *The Invention of Autonomy: A History of Modern Moral Philosophy*. Cambridge: Cambridge University Press.

Shaftesbury, A. A. C. (2001 [1711]) *Characteristicks of Men, Manners, Opinions, Times*. Edited by D. J. den Uyl. 3 vols. Indianapolis: Liberty Fund.

Sheridan, P. (2006) 'Introduction'. In *Philosophical Writings, by Catharine Trotter Cockburn*, edited by P. Sheridan. Peterborough, ON: Broadview Press.

Sheridan, P. (2007) 'Reflection, Nature, and Moral Law: The Extent of Catharine Cockburn's Lockeanism in Her Defence of Mr. Locke's Essay'. *Hypatia* 22 (3):133–51.

Sheridan, P. (2018a) 'On Catharine Trotter Cockburn's Metaphysics of Morality'. In *Early Modern Women on Metaphysics*, edited by E. Thomas, 247–65. Cambridge: Cambridge University Press.

Sheridan, P. (2018b) 'Virtue, Affection, and the Social Good: The Moral Philosophy of Catharine Trotter Cockburn and the Bluestockings'. *Philosophy Compass* 13 (3):e12478.

Sheridan, P. (2022) 'Locke and Catharine Trotter Cockburn'. In *The Lockean Mind*, edited by J. Gordon-Roth and S. Weinberg, 27–32. Abingdon, UK: Routledge.

Stuart-Buttle, T. (2019) *From Moral Theology to Moral Philosophy: Cicero and Visions of Humanity*. Oxford: Oxford University Press.

Sund, E. M. K. A. (2013) 'Catharine Trotter Cockburn's Moral Philosophy'. PhD Dissertation, Monash University.

Tabb, K. (2019) 'Locke on Enthusiasm and the Association of Ideas'. In *Oxford Studies in Early Modern Philosophy*, edited by D. Rutherford, 75–104. Oxford: Oxford University Press.

Tabb, K. (2022) 'Habituation and the Association of Ideas in Locke's Developmental Psychology'. In *The Lockean Mind*, edited by J. Gordon-Roth and S. Weinberg, 385–95. Abingdon, UK: Routledge.

Thiel, U. (2011) *The Early Modern Subject: Self-Consciousness and Personal Identity from Descartes to Hume*. Oxford: Oxford University Press.

Thiel, U. (2012) 'Religion and Materialist Metaphysics: Some Aspects of the Debate about the Resurrection of the Body in Eighteenth-Century Britain'. In *Philosophy and Religion in Enlightenment Britain: New Case Studies*, edited by R. Savage, 90–111. Oxford: Oxford University Press.

Thomas, E. (2013) 'Catharine Cockburn on Substantival Space'. *History of Philosophy Quarterly* 30 (3):195–214.

Thomas, E. (2015) 'Catharine Cockburn on Unthinking Immaterial Substance: Souls, Space, and Related Matters'. *Philosophy Compass* 10 (4):255–63.

Thomas, E. (2017) 'Creation, Divine Freedom, and Catharine Cockburn: An Intellectualist on Possible Worlds and Contingent Laws'. In *Women and Liberty, 1600–1800: Philosophical Essays*, edited by J. Broad and K. Detlefsen, 206–20. Oxford: Oxford University Press.

Thomas, E. (2018) *Absolute Time: Rifts in Early Modern British Metaphysics*. Oxford: Oxford University Press.

Toland, J. (2013 [1704]) *Letters to Serena*. Edited by I. Leask. Dublin: Four Courts Press.

Tuckness, A. (1999) 'The Coherence of a Mind: John Locke and the Law of Nature'. *Journal of the History of Philosophy* 37 (1):73–90.

Waithe, M. E., ed. (1987–95) *A History of Women Philosophers*. 4 vols. Dordrecht: Kluwer Academic Publishers.

Walmsley, J. C., H. Craig, and J. Burrows. (2016) 'The Authorship of the *Remarks upon an Essay Concerning Humane Understanding*'. *Eighteenth-Century Thought* 6:205–43.

Warburton, W. (1738) *The Divine Legation of Moses Demonstrated, on the Principles of a Religious Deist, from the Omission of the Doctrine of a Future State of Reward and Punishment in the Jewish Dispensation*. London: Printed for F. Gyles.

Ward, R. W. (1995) 'Divine Will, Natural Law and the Voluntarism/ Intellectualism Debate in Locke'. *History of Political Thought* 16 (2):208–18.

Warren, H. C. (1921) *A History of the Association Psychology from Hartley to Lewes*. Baltimore: Charles Scribner's Sons.

Watts, I. (1733) *Philosophical Essays on Various Subjects*. London: Printed for R. Ford and R. Hett.

Winkler, K. P. (1991) 'Locke on Personal Identity'. *Journal of the History of Philosophy* 29 (2):201–26.

Yolton, J. W. (1983) *Thinking Matter: Materialism in Eighteenth-Century Britain*. Minneapolis: University of Minnesota Press.

Acknowledgements

I owe special thanks to Jacqueline Broad for inviting me to write this book on Catharine Trotter Cockburn and for all her encouragement and helpful advice along the way. I am grateful for the helpful comments that I received from two anonymous reviewers. Space constraints did not allow me to address all the excellent comments with as much depth as may be desirable, but I hope to develop my views further in future research. I would also like to thank Donald Ainslie, Miranda Anderson, Anita van der Bos, Sofía Calvente, Graham Clay, Evie Filea, M. Folescu, Jörn Müller, Dominik Perler, Sonja Schierbaum, Stephan Schmid, Kylie Shahar, Natalia Strok, Aaron Wells, and the members of an online Cockburn reading group for helpful discussions of Cockburn's philosophy and feedback and comments on my work. I presented my research on Cockburn at the Institute for Advanced Studies in the Humanities at the University of Edinburgh, the Society and Human Nature in Early Modern Philosophy Workshop at the University of St Andrews, the University of Würzburg, the 2021 British Society for the History of Philosophy Women in the History of Philosophy Conference, the 2021 John Locke Conference, the 2021 Travelling Early Modern Philosophy Organization Conference, the Varieties of Voluntarism in Medieval and Early Modern Ethics Online Conference, and the Virtual Early Modern Philosophy Work-in-Progress Workshop and would like to thank the audiences at these events for helpful feedback. I wrote substantial parts of this book during a research visit as American Philosophical Association Fellow at the Institute for Advanced Studies in the Humanities at the University of Edinburgh during the summer of 2022. I would like to thank the Institute for Advanced Studies in the Humanities for their hospitality and wonderful research environment, and the American Philosophical Association for offering me the fellowship for this research visit. I would also like to acknowledge the support of a University College Dublin Seed Funding Career Development Award, which enabled me to pursue new research on early modern women philosophers.

Cambridge Elements ⁼

Women in the History of Philosophy

Jacqueline Broad
Monash University

Jacqueline Broad is Professor of Philosophy at Monash University, Australia. Her area of expertise is early modern philosophy, with a special focus on seventeenth and eighteenth-century women philosophers. She is the author of *Women Philosophers of the Seventeenth Century* (Cambridge University Press, 2002), *A History of Women's Political Thought in Europe, 1400–1700* (with Karen Green; Cambridge University Press, 2009), and *The Philosophy of Mary Astell: An Early Modern Theory of Virtue* (Oxford University Press, 2015).

Advisory Board

Dirk Baltzly, *University of Tasmania*
Sandrine Bergès, *Bilkent University*
Marguerite Deslauriers, *McGill University*
Karen Green, *University of Melbourne*
Lisa Shapiro, *McGill University*
Emily Thomas, *Durham University*

About the Series

In this Cambridge Elements series, distinguished authors provide concise and structured introductions to a comprehensive range of prominent and lesser-known figures in the history of women's philosophical endeavour, from ancient times to the present day.

Cambridge Elements ≡

Women in the History of Philosophy

Elements in the Series

A full series listing is available at: www.cambridge.org/EWHP

Printed in the United States
by Baker & Taylor Publisher Services
Printed in the United States
by Baker & Taylor Publisher Services